THE AUTOBIOGRAPHY of **WAYNE B PEACOCK**

WAYNE B PEACOCK, BSME

authorHOUSE

AuthorHouse™
1663 Liberty Drive
Bloomington, IN 47403
www.authorhouse.com
Phone: 1 (800) 839-8640

© 2018 Wayne B Peacock, BSME. All rights reserved.
Cover Model: Wayne Peacock

No part of this book may be reproduced, stored in a retrieval system, or transmitted by any means without the written permission of the author.

Published by AuthorHouse 12/07/2018

ISBN: 978-1-5462-6644-0 (sc)
ISBN: 978-1-5462-6643-3 (hc)
ISBN: 978-1-5462-6642-6 (e)

Library of Congress Control Number: 2018913022

Print information available on the last page.

Any people depicted in stock imagery provided by Getty Images are models, and such images are being used for illustrative purposes only.
Certain stock imagery © Getty Images.

This book is printed on acid-free paper.

Because of the dynamic nature of the Internet, any web addresses or links contained in this book may have changed since publication and may no longer be valid. The views expressed in this work are solely those of the author and do not necessarily reflect the views of the publisher, and the publisher hereby disclaims any responsibility for them.

Scripture quotations marked KJV are from the Holy Bible, King James Version (Authorized Version). First published in 1611. Quoted from the KJV Classic Reference Bible, Copyright © 1983 by The Zondervan Corporation.

NKJV
NIV
NLT

To my parents,
Ben and Florence Peacock,
who served love for breakfast,
lunch and dinner,
topped with a goodnight kiss
for my brother Dale and me.

You must make the effort yourself. The masters only point the way.
The Buddha

CONTENTS

Purpose xi
Foreword xiii
Preface xvii

Part I Introductions

Chapter One: The Early Years and Before 1
Chapter Two: Dale Gilbert Peacock 5
Chapter Three: Birth, Horoscopes, Myers-Briggs and
    Enneagrams 8
Chapter Four: Games, Pets, Near Tragedies, Choirboy,
    Hoyt Pool and Dental Care 11
Chapter Five: Underwood Memorial Baptist Church 20

Part II - The Main Events 1938-1973

Chapter Six: Wauwatosa: The Setting, Parenting, Schooling &
    Athletics 23
Chapter Seven: Hal Peck 34
Chapter Eight: Green Bay Packers 37
Chapter Nine: First Racket, Tennis Results, Tony Trabert 41
Chapter Ten: University of Michigan & Beta Theta Pi 49
Chapter Eleven: Military Service 60
Chapter Twelve: Marriage and Children 63
Chapter Thirteen: Factory Mutual 80
Chapter Fourteen: Allendale Insurance 90

Chapter Fifthteen: New England Patriots 100
Chapter Sixteen: The World of Fine Arts 104
Chapter Seventeen: Road Racing 107
Chapter Eighteen: Posits 117
Chapter Nineteen: The Epilogue 118

Acknowledgements 121
About the Author 123

PURPOSE

To live life to the fullest and to share my
gifts unselfishly with the universe.

This biography will serve as one means of manifesting that purpose.

FOREWORD

In 1971 I was two years out of university and working for the British government, carrying out research into materials used in ballistic missile reentry vehicles. The work was interesting enough but the skills I was acquiring hardly seemed transferable unless I defected to the USSR. There were plenty of outside opportunities for graduates at that time and after a short interview I found myself a trainee loss prevention engineer at FM Insurance in London, the overseas arm of the North American Factory Mutual System. I had been told that the concept was that by investing money in world class loss prevention Factory Mutual clients benefited from low insurance rates and the services of a team of loss prevention engineers. It seemed a sound idea and one that intrigued me.

My first few days in the London office as one of these engineers were not the measured, organised calm that I might have expected from a traditional British insurance company. The organisation was experiencing massive growth in insuring the overseas subsidiaries of Fortune 500 companies and although the loss prevention engineers had plenty of data sheets, manuals and "Practice and Procedure" documents that specified what to do, we were often left to our own devices in working out how to actually do it in the world outside North America. Desks were in short supply and it wasn't unusual to come into the office in the morning and find "your" desk occupied by a German or French engineer who flatly refused to move!! You would be given a week's work anywhere in the world, comprising a few addresses claimed to be factories and their telephone numbers and then expected to organise your own itinerary, book your hotels and advise the customer when you would be arriving. All this was done using only telex and a telephone system that required you to call the International Operator, book a call and wait to be connected at some later time.

It was during this period that I first met Wayne. He was one of the senior engineers and stood out in my eyes as he seemed to be one of the few sane, competent and sober ones. To try and cope with the rapid expansion overseas the American management had asked all their existing North American offices for volunteers to live in London on assignment and offered a healthy cash incentive. The results were a mixed bag. A few of them including Wayne were motivated by the chance of living overseas and experiencing travel and new cultures. Some were motivated more by the money and used the slackness of the travel and expense system to add even more to their bank account. Others were by and large encouraged to leave North America by their local managers and "make a new start away from the problems at home". One such expatriate left the USA drunk, drank more on the plane and simply disappeared when he reached London. It was weeks before we tracked him down.

I was a relatively young engineer who had worked only in a slow paced, hierarchical government service and the environment was a considerable challenge. Without the support, advice and friendship that Wayne gave, I would not have stayed and that would have meant missing out on a twenty year career with FM that ranks as some of the best times in my working life. Even though I eventually moved on in the 1990's, I still consider the early years with FM to be a model for how an organisation can become effective from a fractious beginning and how a job can be a passion and fulfilling.

The first thing Wayne did was to convince me and other new engineers that what we were doing was worthwhile. He had a passion for loss prevention engineering and wanted to share that passion with anyone who would listen. We truly felt that the aim of the Factory Mutual System, reducing losses in industry and commerce by superior engineering, was important, was economically sound and would benefit the clients. Wayne constantly reinforced that core value of our belief system and it became a commitment that we all shared and that bound us together.

What was even more important however was that he made us realise that we could make a difference as individuals. We were a team but that team needed every member to be committed to the core beliefs and determined to do their individual best. When I first joined FMI I was unsure of my ability to work all over the world, unsure of my capabilities and certainly unsure that I wanted to work in such a chaotic environment. Wayne understood that and set me the task of changing it and changing myself too. He had faith in me, he set me challenges and he supported me while I found my own ways of meeting them. If things went wrong, the question was "Why?". We would attack the failure and understand what went wrong, why it failed and what did we need to do it better next time. But if it went well, there was still the question to be asked "Why not better?". Why accept a success without understanding if you can't be even more successful next time. He taught me to understand my strengths, to use them fully and to never be content with the status quo.

Whatever Wayne does, he does to his fullest ability. He was a top rated junior tennis player, a successful manager and engineer and a dedicated runner in later life. To say merely that he seeks perfection is to miss the point. He aims to do his best in every avenue that is open to him, to try new things and succeed in them, to enthuse others with the same desire, to teach us all that whatever you do, do it as well as you can because otherwise, why would you do it?

From the 1990's onward I never worked with Wayne again although we have always remained good friends but the lessons he instilled in me still remain. Always do your best, be sure in your own abilities and push them to the limit, stand up for what you know to be right, don't be ashamed to have a passion in your life and most importantly never accept that today's best can't be bettered.

Wayne's journey through life has been varied and he has always been looking for "the answer" to his questions about life. This book may not give you the answers to your life but I bet that by reading it you will find the tools that help you find your own answers and if it does, Wayne B. Peacock will be happy.

PREFACE

Cogitating on the past is one of my favorite pastimes. Reliving and savoring the past with its poignant lessons became so engrossing, I decided to write my autobiography so that when my memory fades away, as I am told is inevitable, I will have my life story in writing to help me recall what was most important to me. I had in mind a collection of stories for each major element of my life. The stories would reflect the perpetual curiosity, optimistic outlook, playfulness and can-do attitude of an adventuresome biography as well as his accomplishments and failures.

To get the ball rolling, I identified six major elements of my life for my autobiography. Over time, the list grew to eighteen. I decided to cover my first sixty years in eleven elements in Part One and leave the remaining seven elements for the Part 2 book.

1
The Early Years and Before

I want to share a dark heritage story. Our family inherited an alcoholic gene from our Norwegian heritage. My mother, Florence, was of Norwegian heritage. She was born into a family where her father and three of her four brothers were alcoholics. Thus, her sister Mabel and she were adult children of alcoholics with a heavy burden to carry. I can only imagine how much my mom feared having a child who might follow in her father's footsteps; enter my brother Dale Gilbert Peacock. As Dale grew into his thirties, my mom must have recognized the indicators of alcoholism. And yet, she nurtured and loved Dale as he was and was not. She might have qualified as an enabler, however cruel and unfair that might come across. Sadly, Dale died tragically and prematurely one day before his 40th birthday. Reportedly, he was found dead on a San Francisco street. To the best of our knowledge, he had spent his final years drinking and gambling on container ships going back and forth between California and Japan He confirmed this life style in his frequent letters.

His heart-struck father flew to California to identify the body and accompany him home to Wauwatosa, where he lay in rest at the Schmidt & Bartlett Funeral Home. The volume of visitors was enormous. The guest book entries said it all about Dale's legacy. He had made friends everywhere he ventured. The burial service followed at the bucolic family plot in Big Bend, WI. The only time I ever saw my dad weep was just prior to Dale's casket being lowered into the gravesite. That most poignant of images will remain in my heart and consciousness forever.

My parents were Benjamin Noyes Peacock and Florence Gilbert Peacock. My mother's parents came to America from Norway on a sailing ship. My father's English forbearers arrived in New England in the 19th century. Both parents were born and raised on a farm: my father in Wisconsin, my mother in North Dakota. They lived through World War I, the Great Depression, World War II, the Korean War and Vietnam War.

When I qualified in the Rhode Island State Senior Olympics in 2008, it led me, as serendipity would have it, to learning more about my heritage and ancestors. I competed in the 2009 National Senior Games at Stanford University. My age group was 70-74. The track race was 1500 meters and the road races were 5K and 10Ks. I went to the starting lines with great confidence, knowing that I had put my all into the weeks and months of preparation. In a very competitive field against many of the country's best runners, I brought home one sixth-place and two 7th-place ribbons. My pride was obvious each time I stood on the podium with my ribbon.

As a perk for the contestants, several companies were offering free products and services. One such company was 23andme, a privately held personal genomics and biotechnological company based in Mountain View, CA. The company is named for the twenty three pairs of chromosomes in a human cell. They were offering a revolutionary DNA test in exchange for samples of my saliva. The following is one of their many findings:

Ancestry Composition

- Wayne Peacock 100%
- European 100%
- Northwestern European 99.4%
    Scandinavian 44.6%
    Portuguese & Irish 29.9%
    French & German 2.8%
    Broadly Northwestern European 23.0%

There was nothing in this Ancestry Composition that surprised me.

One of my father's many hobbies was tracing his descendants. He spent countless hours drawing up charts of his and my mom's ancestors. For him, it may have been a puzzle, for which he worked to put together as much of the whole picture as he could. Each confirmed step back in history brought a new level of satisfaction. He would have found 23 and me a powerful tool, as he was anything but a Luddite.

He had traced back to an ancestor named William Noyes, who was said to have been the Rector of the Parish Church of St. Nicholas in the tiny village of Cholderton, England. The problem was that he could never find Cholderton on any maps, which frustrated him no end. Then one year he and my mom came to visit us in Putney Heath, southwest of London, where we lived for the eight years before returning to the states. One morning he came bounding into the breakfast room to tell us that he had finally found Cholderton on a map. In no time, we all crammed into our tiny (Dutch) DAF automobile. The DAF was unique in that it featured a continuously variable rubber belt driven transmission system.

We arrived in Cholderton, or more properly West Cholderton, to find the exhaustively searched- for Parish Church of St. Nicholas. My dad stood in front of the church taking in the moment for a long time. He found a small table upon entering. On the table was an 18 inch gold cross with the names of all former rectors etched on the flat base. The first name was William Noyes, 1601. Bingo! My dad's two decades-long challenge was met and with a "splendid" ending, as the Brits would say. I took several photos of my effusive parents outside in front of the church. One of those keepsake photos hung on a beam in our East Greenwich basement for the life of our time there. It was a testament to my father's diligence and perseverance.

2
Dale Gilbert Peacock

Dale was born in Big Bend on September 5, 1931, seven years before I came into the picture. His parents moved to Wauwatosa in 1936, where he attended grade, junior and high school. He, like me, inherited a high IQ from my intelligent parents. He was rebellious and a one-of-a-kind. The Cardinal Pennant "54" yearbook photo shows him in a classroom with a cigarette behind his ear, even though he wasn't a smoker.

He gambled on anything and everything, from dice, sheepshead, poker, pool, bumper pool and billiards. For example, I was scheduled to play Bobby Stuckert, the reigning Wisconsin state men's champion, in the finals of the Wisconsin State Open Tennis Championships in Wauwatosa's City Park. He told me he was going to see what odds he could get from Las Vegas. Hmm. As I never heard more about it, I assume he lost his cell phone. That is unfortunate, because upsetting Bobby Stuckert the next day was the biggest accomplishment of my young tennis career. Also, it may say something about Dale's precience.

Social norms, conventions, rules, regulations and laws were there to be broken, which he made a practice of doing in a kind, playful and eccentric manner. A perfect example happened in his senior year when he and two others acquired a pig, greased it up and pushed it through the door of the gymnasium where two thousand cheering fans were watching a Tosa basketball game. That tells you all you need to know about the ingenuity and range of his pranksterisms.

Everytime I talk with Joyce Elliott, a very close and favorite cousin, she relates more Dale stories, and always with a big smile on her face. Joyce would end up by saying, "Dale was quite a guy!" She had nothing but love for Dale, as would be seconded by countless friends and acquaintances.

Dale was a very good tennis player. As a fifteen year old, he was ranked number one in Wisconsin. He played number two singles on his dads 1947 Suburban Conference winning tennis team. Then his dad choose Joe Been to play number two singles in the Wisconsin state meet the following week. While I was not close to the situation, I recall some understandingly hard feelings on Dales part, as what probably felt like a demotion. Knowing my dads moral compass, I assume that Joe had earned the promotion.

Just recently, I found this hand written note in Dale's 1947 Cardinal Pennant: "Dale, stay away from all the wild woman and cigarettes and you'd be state champion." Wasted talent? Hmm.

Dale went to the University of Wisconsin for a few years and eventually graduated at the University of Wisconsin-Milwaukee around 1957. I say eventually, because Dale spent three years in the US Army where he became a much honored paratrooper. Talk about guts and courage; Dale was all man.

As to man-woman relationships, there was one span of time when he was living in Wauwatosa, and had a girlfriend named Ruth Paulus. I found a keepsake photo of them being happy together on a couch.

I was sad when Dale died. I mourned, but don't recall any specific feelings and emotions. The seven year age difference and the reality that our lives seldom meshed, impacted the depth of my mourning. I do know that I inherited my dad's non-reactive and drama-free traits.

3
Birth, Horoscopes, Myers-Briggs and Enneagrams

I was born 2:02 am on July 23, 1938 at the Deaconess Hospital in Milwaukee, WI. This date determined my birthstone to be a red ruby. The 8 lbs ½ oz brown haired and blue eyed me was listed as "lively" on the Disposition and Behavior Report. My first bottled formula was 6 oz. of water, 6 oz. of milk with two level teaspoons of dextra maltose No. 1.

I have been a fan of Horoscopes ever since I learned that I fell under the Zodiac sign of Leo, which originates from the constellation of Leo. The symbol of the Leo is the Lion. A Leo personality is bold, intelligent, warm and courageous. A Leo is a natural leader ready to blaze a trail, vanquish injustice, and make a name for themselves along the way. Leos are also an ambitious lot, and their strength of purpose allows them to accomplish a great deal. If I had been born one hundred and two minutes earlier, my sign would have been Cancer. The first three primary Cancer traits are loyalty, deep intuition and sentimentality. Taken as a whole, the Leo and Cancer traits have proved to be remarkably prescient, i.e. predictive of my life's stories, of which you will be reading. Every morning I read my Leo horoscope, follow with the Cancer, and then ponder about which fits best. Occasionally, I will clip out one Horoscope, attach it to my PC and take comfort or inspiration throughout the day.

Sourcing from *Please Understand Me*, my well worn bible for the Myers-Briggs typing system, I am an ENTP. ENTPs prefer extroversion to introversion, intuition to sensation, thinking to feeling and perceiving to judging. They are imaginative and enthusiastic and often a source of inspiration. ENTPs tend to be fascinating conversationalists. Characteristically, they have an eye out for a better way and are on the lookout for new projects and activities. They often bring a fresh approach to their work and their lives. "It can't be done" is a challenge to the ENTP. I got quite familiar with the sixteen different types and found it to be a useful addition to my knowledge of human beings and their temperaments. *Please Understand Me* is on my Hall of Fame bookshelf.

To illustrate the high value of being hip with Myers-Briggs, I offer a telling story. My wife Morlean and I were out for a Friday night fish fry with our fellow Wauwatosa classmates. Post fish fry and beers, we visited a downtown bar on the Milwaukee River, as was the custom in Milwaukee, the home of Miller High Life, Schlitz, Blatz and Pabst beers.

After two of drinks, Morlean was ready to go home. I brushed her off by calling her a party pooper. At the time I did recognize her as an Introvert. Introverts lose energy in a crowd. The crowd was sapping her energy, where as I and other extroverts were gaining energy. Out of ignorance, I was being inconsiderate. Regardless of the introvert/extrovert combo, I made it about me and my wants. Unfortunately, on some things you don't get a do-over. Darn. I would make up for her in after-life were it not for my atheistic knowing that there is no afterlife. It's just over.

The *Enneagram* (pronounced ANY-a-gram) is a study of the nine basic types of people. Ennea is Greek for the number nine, and gram means "a drawing with nine points." It is represented by a circle containing a nine-pointed starlike shape.

The roots of the Enneagram go back many centuries. Its exact origin is not known, but it is believed to have been taught orally in secret Sufi brotherhoods in the Middle East. The Russian mystical teacher G. I. Gurdjieff introduced it to Europe in the 1920s, and it arrived in the United States in the 1960s.

The tool can help us with self examination. It explains why we behave the way we do, and it points to specific directions for individual growth. It is a valuable tool for improving relationships with family, friends and coworkers. I have enjoyed a remarkable amount of pleasure from the Enneagram ever since I discovered it many years ago, and the gift keeps on giving.

I am an Enneagram One, sometimes labeled The Reformer.

Reformers are realistic and that is me. I take pride in seeing things as they are and are not. Reformers are conscientious and I am nothing if not conscientious; sometimes going overboard with accuracy, for example. Reformers strive to live up to their high ideals, a trait which I exemplify by responding positively to my sense of right and wrong. Ones are motivated by the need to live their life the right way, including improving themselves and the world around them. Cross out "Ones" and insert "Wayne" and you've seen my inner job description.

Ones at their best are ethical, reliable, productive, wise, idealistic, fair, honest, orderly, self-disciplined and have a good sense of humor.

Ones at their worst are judgmental, inflexible, dogmatic, critical of others, overly serious, controlling, anxious and jealous. Reformers see anger as a character flaw and try to hold it back. It is common for anger to be masked in kidding and sarcasm.

In 2017 I attended a five day Enneagram Workshop at the Omega Institute for Holistic Studies at Rhinebeck, NY. It was my first visit there since 1994. It was well worth the time, cost and effort. It served as a valuable time-out from my head centered routines.

In one of my Life Coaching Training classes there was an exercise wherein classmates would vote on which one of seven possible types you are, after watching you perform a five minute improv skit on stage. The highest number of votes saw me as a "Beauty"; the next highest a "Charm" and the third highest an "Eccentric." Beauties are warm and inviting. Charms are only slightly different. Eccentrics are what the name implies.

Sandra Lipsey, a fellow life coach, and I talk every Thursday afternoon at 4:30. She knows me inside and out and is very conversant with the Beauty, Charm and Eccentric definitions and how the class had voted me. With no hesitation, she asserts that I am currently living the life of an Eccentric. I agree with her.

4

Games, Pets, Near Tragedies, Choirboy, Hoyt Pool and Dental Care

*And a voice said: "Come, jump into the river of
life with me and swim like hell."
And the student replied: "I'm all in"
Guess what? The student has been doing it for 80 years*

Games were at the center of "Wayne's World" from day one. I welcomed the challenges that games present, as without challenges, they would not be games. An early memory has a little girl and I playing a game of marbles on our hands and knees in my backyard. Each of us was trying our best to capture the other's marbles. It was friendly, yet intensive, even as seven-year-old children. This innocent playground scenario illuminates three basic facts of life. First, we are born with a competitive gene. Second, if you want something, you have to go get it, as no one is going to get it to you. Third, we have to learn from our shortcomings and mistakes as well as our triumphs.

As a corollary to the preceding proffer, what I learned playing marbles in my backyard would inure to my athletic endeavors, education, career, relationships and most important of all, his happiness.

The number of accessible competitive games grew rapidly with each having its own attraction. I played kick the can, hide and seek, kickball on my street and would throw a basketball ball at a basket in my driveway/backyard. Then came softball, hardball and football. In one hardball game at City Park, I was playing second base when a batter hit a high fly ball in my direction. I caught it, but at the expense of a broken fourth finger on my right hand.

It was at the Village Inn where I was first exposed to the utility and fun of dice games. Dale and Tom Fischer, the owner and bartender of the Village Inn, would throw dice to determine who would pay for the drinks Dale consumed. The Village Inn also had a Bumper Pool table at which Dale's and my friends played by the hours, and they always included placing bets, even if only a shekel or two. Poker, sheepshead, and other card games became central to both Dale's social existence and my own.

I played several years of fast pitch softball on my brother's Village Inn sponsored teams. The uniforms made us look like we were big leaguers. At one time or another, I played catcher, first base, second base, third base and left field. Typically, I was chosen to be leadoff batter. I tried all sorts of machinations to get on base, from bunting down the third base line so the third baseman would have a longer throw to first base, to dragging a bunt down the first based line. In one late summer game, I made a diving, head over heels catch in left field and the next week I hit my only home run on one of the first couple pitches of the game. A recent discovery in a pile of old newspaper clippings, was that I had hit over four-hundred per cent in one season. Holy moly, that was Ty Cobb like. All of the above play was in addition to my Mckinley Park Tennis Team matches and frequent weekend tennis tournaments.

Along with my athletics, I had an affinity for all kinds of pets, just like I have an affinity for all types of people. The people and pets I like best are those with welcoming personalities. Who wants to fear a pet or have a pet who scares strangers. Learning about a new pets personality is the interesting bit. A dog and cat can show their love and appreciation for you a hundred times a day, especially at meal time. A goldfish and a canary allow you to watch them get excited at meal times. A turtle acts as if you don't exist and seldom cracks a smile.

My first pet was Christina, a white Persian Longhair cat. She had a round face and short muzzle. Characteristically, she was dignified, docile, quiet and sweet. She enjoyed being held and would often sleep at the end of my bed. My memory recalls no downsides, such as bringing home dead mice. I loved her. She loved me.

My next pets were domesticated yellow canaries. Canaries are a small songbird in the Finch family originating from the Macaronesian Islands. Male canaries can mimic sounds such as telephone ringtones and door bell chimes, but only if they hear these sounds while young. Strange, I never thought of naming my birds. It would have enhanced my pet experience, if not the birds. Is it unrealistic for the canaries to have taken umbrage at being unnamed?

My first canary found its way out of its cage and flew out an open window, all because of my carelessness. The same thing happened with my second and final try at having to take care of a tiny winged pet.

My third pets were goldfish, a freshwater fish in the family Cyprinidae. A relatively small member of the carp family, the goldfish is native to East Asia. Our goldfish came in orange, black and white. Overfeeding, underfeeding and not maintaining a clean tank brought our attempt at having an aquarium end one day after I buried the last two surviving fish. The moral of the goldfish story is that parents can not depend on teenage promises to do their chores.

When I was eleven, my favorite pet was Nicky, a common mid-size breed, the name of which I can't recall. Nicky belonged to Billy Olson, a neighbor three doors away. Billy was seven years my senior, and a close friend of my brother Dale. Nicky may as well have been mine, what with all the time we spent together. I did a lot of taking care of Nicky, including two-to-three hour long adventures in Hoyt Park.

One of the many bizarre things I learned from Billy was trapping gophers. He would fill up a pail with river water, pour it down a gopher hole and collect the drenched golfer in Billy's Custom Designed Gopher Trap. Billy released some gophers, but others perished as a result of Nicky's instinctual behavior. I freed some gophers when my better self took charge. With the twentieth century's wildlife conservation practices, the practice of trapping gophers would not be listed as a sport, nor would it show up by Googling. Billy Olson and his young sidekick may have been the only two gopher trappers in all of history.

On a positive note, Billy taught me how to shoot my first real gun in his basement range. It was a German Luger pistol. Shooting something other than a play gun brought me fully alive.

Billy left his mark on me in another way, pun intended. Occasionally, he would give me a ride on his motorcycle. It was thrilling and scary at the same time. I would hold on with all my might. Once I got off the bike and feeling a pain on my right leg, I looked down and discovered a three-inch-long burn on the inside of my right ankle. Some seven decades later, the conversation-starting scar has faded but is still visible.

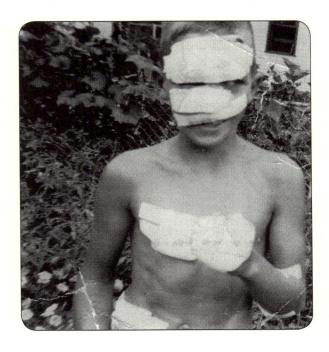

My first near tragedy occured on a bright sunny morning when I was ten years old. I went for a long ride on the bike that Dale passed down to me. I peddled up to the top of 86th Street, then took a right on Stickney Avenue and road all the way to 76th Street where I turned left for one block to North Avenue. That left me at the top of a fairly steep hill. I was picking up speed as I raced down the hill, when the bike's frame suddenly collapsed. I was thrown to the pavement and rendered unconscious. I incurred a concussion and scraped and bloodied face, chest, hips, hands, knees and just about everything else. A conscientious truck driver picked me up and took me to a clinic a mile down the road. An ambulance transported me to the Milwaukee County Hospital where they removed the embedded gravel from my forehead with a wire brush and green soap. The wire brush clean-ups were by far the most painful experiences I had ever had. The truck driver reported that he barely missed hitting me. One lesson that can be drawn from my accident is that I was too young to be driving so fast on such a steep and dangerous hill. A second lesson I learned was never to drive an old bike unless it's had a safety check.

In the listless summer of 1958, between tennis tournaments and fast pitch softball, the Village Inn became a harbinger for a second near-death experience. I was drinking at the bar with my brother Dale at the Village Inn one afternoon when I got the hare-brained idea of challenging him to a race of who could drink fifteen shots of gin the fastest. So Tom Fischer, the bartender, an insanely naive and irresponsible guy, enabled my near-death experience when he filled up thirteen shot glasses with pure alcohol and lined them up in front of Dale and me. I started chugging them down, one right after another as if it were water. After I had downed the twelfth shot, I passed out and fell to the floor unconscious. The fire department was called. They rushed me to the Milwaukee County Hospital where the attending doctor stated that if it weren't for my exceedingly strong heart, I would have been dead. The next morning I was released from the hospital and kindly driven to the Wauwatosa Police Department by two officers. Once there, I was formally arrested on a charge of being "plain drunk". Come to think of it, I never paid Dale for my losing the thirteen-shot bet.

One of my best friends, Al Schmatzhagen, picked me up from the police station and drove me to his home, where I had been living in their basement. I will go out on a limb and say that I had a very sound night's sleep. The next morning I flew to Detroit with a class five hangover to be best man in my frat brother Bob Quarnstrom's wedding. As the wedding bells began to ring, I was sitting in the basement of the church trying to think of how I could entertain everyone with my best man speech, which I planned to give as a tongue-in-cheek condolence theme. I came up with a clever take on the path to Bob and Karen's union. I began with, "Bob and I were fixed up with two high school seniors, Karen and her best friend, Midge Stockard, for the Michigan State - Michigan game in Lansing. The weekend was unremarkable, which should be interpreted that at most we got a sole good night peck on the cheek. When we got home, Bob asked if I would trade his date for mine, who was Karen. I agreed to the trade but expected something tangible in return; like a hot date, for example. He never did pay up. It has been hard to forgive and forget.

I became addicted to the morning Milwaukee Sentinel Sports Page when I was ten. In the warm months, my interest was focused on the batting averages of the Milwaukee Brewers. In the winter months, picture me in my PJs and on my hands and knees beside the heating vent coming up from the basement furnace. My obsession for reading the sports section first thing in the morning is still in play. Simply scratch out the Milwaukee Brewers, Green Bay Packers and Wisconsin Badgers and insert the Boston Red Sox, Boston Celtics, New England Patriots and Michigan Wolverines as my current teams.

What with all of the shenanigans surrounding my youth, no one would ever call me a choirboy. However, for the eleventh and twelfth years of my life, I was every bit a choirboy. How so, you might wonder? You can blame it on Dean Randell, who was the choir director at the Episcopal Church in downtown Milwaukee. Between Dean and my parents I was cajoled into being a choirboy. It meant that when Dean beeped his car horn for me on Thursday afternoons at the Lincoln Grade School playground, I had to drop whatever I was doing so he could drive me to choir practice sixteen miles away. Choir practice wasn't something I enjoyed at all, although I did make seventy five cents for the three hours I was transported out of Wayne's World of Fun and Play.

Our choir practiced Handel's Messiah for the three months preceding Easter Sunday. During the middle of the Easter performance, I had to go "big" time. The crude pun is intended. Big was slang for number two in the Peacock household. I did not have the presence of mind nor the courage to get up and repose in the bathroom. As a consequence, I had some "big" time discomfort during the remainder of the seemingly endless service. I know that story stinks, but I had to tell it.

No history of my youth would be complete without the Hoyt Park Swimming Pool Stories. The pool is the centerpiece of the beautiful Menominee River Parkway that runs through Wauwatosa. This outdoor pool is enormous. It has two high diving boards, four low boards and a baby pool. Confidentially, I never had the nerve to dive off the high dive.

From early in my life, at nine-years-old I would run the third of a mile to the pool for both morning and afternoon sessions. I would be in the pool for six to seven hours a day and sunbathing on the warm concrete the rest of the time. The accumulation of hundreds of hours of pool time qualified me as a water person. But I always did and always will hate getting into cold water. I don't know if my absence of fat is relevant or not.

Alongside of the pool were trailer homes, placed there in World War II. Marcella Hall, who lived in one of the trailers, and I swam and played around together. Our friendship grew into my first puppy love. The puppy love lasted a year or so until her family moved away. A warm memory remains some seventy years later.

Hoyt Pool was my home away from home in the summer. It was also the place where I had asked, and sometimes pleaded, with my dad to come down and watch me swim. I chose a specific spot along the fence where he would have the best sight line. When he arrived one afternoon, I jumped out of the pool to give him placement instructions. I dove in and swam as fast as I could; then looked up to see him turned away and talking with someone else. Ouch! It was one of those scenes in life that has stayed with me.

Les Hartfield, father of one of the high school tennis team members, was a Grand Master at duplicate bridge. He took me under his wing, gave me a new Gorin lesson sheet each week and took me to a couple of competitive bridge tournaments. At tournaments you can win master points. In the few tournaments I entered, I won two or three master points, and was justly proud. While I have not played bridge for forty or fifty years, I have read the bridge column in the Providence Journal newspaper every weekday, right after reading my Leo and Cancer Horoscopes.

The older I get, the more grateful I am for the countless gifts I inherited from my parents. They provided the love, support and environment for all of my adventures and accomplishments. I couldn't have had better role models, with one exception that I will still be paying for long after you read this. Here is the straight skinny. Mom and Dad did not emphasize the necessity and benefits of brushing my teeth. My theory is that since they both had plates, they were blind to their children's oral needs. And, it was not their nature to be patrolling their kids all day.

In the Peacock home, everyone was on their own, each of us independent when it came to taking care of ourselves. It followed that brushing my teeth was not a priority. As the cavities multiplied, so did my painful experiences in the dentist's chairs. Score one for willful ignorance. It would take a pending date with a sexy girl for me to even consider the desirability of having white teeth and fresh breath. Decades passed without any change in my habits and laziness trumped oral hygiene.

My few remaining teeth exist with the benefit of endless fillings and implants. There might be enough precious metals in my mouth that I'd be smart to itemize this asset in my will. Thankfully, it is not the type of asset that can be passed down from generation to generation.

I recently learned that old fillings contain mercury, which can be a harbinger to memory loss. Now, being much more aware, older and wiser, I will see that those six fillings are replaced. Recently, I saw a poster in my dentist's office which said, *"You don't have to brush all of your teeth, only the ones you wish to keep."* I cop to the likelihood that even if that poster was in all of my previous dental offices, my intrangenance would have prevailed.

The past seventy-two years of preventable suffering has been indescribable. How I could have continued to ignore my toothbrush, even after countless painful sessions in the chair? Certainly, laziness played a major role while my independance gene, by which I mean no one is going to tell me what to do," stole the show. With the money I blew on dentistry, I could have paid for Daniel's and Leslie's grad school years at Oxford or Cambridge. Postscript: I am in a protracted sixteen-month total rebuilding process to compensate for my seventy-eight years of dental care denial.

5
Underwood Memorial Baptist Church

My grandparents were members of the Big Bend Baptist Church and it followed that my parents were married there. I have a keepsake photo of them on the outside steps of the church on their wedding day, July 27, 1927. They were regular church goers and my dad taught adult Sunday School.

When they moved to Wauwatosa in 1933, they joined the Underwood Memorial Baptist Church. My dad became a deacon and church elder, and taught the adult Sunday School. Our family attended Sunday school and the church service that followed until

Dale attended church less and less in his high school years. When I was sixteen, Neil Canter and I became ushers who helped seat the parishioners and passed around the collection plate when it was time. While, sixty-four-years later I can still recite the protestant versions of the widely quoted 23rd Psalm and John 3-16, I did not get much out my relationship with the Baptist Church. My pragmatism made me skeptical about Jesus rising from the dead, the concept of heaven and hell, and other dogma, however it was spun. And besides, play and athletics sparkled brighter than sermons, prayer and hymns.

The Wisconsin Baptist Assembly was established in 1943 and Baptist youth held their first conference the following year in the exquisitely beautiful Green Lake Conference Center. Adjacent to the Center was the highly rated Lawsonia Golf course which ran alongside of Green Lake. I attended a conference in the summer of 1955. One evening, Donna Kunkel agreed to some cuddling in one of the sand traps on the golf course. Our relationship was memorable and it grew into my second puppy love.

After leaving home for college, my interest in attending church lessened until my marriage to Morlean Dowling in the First Unitarian Church in Whitefish Bay. I don't recall when the existence of Unitarianism had caught my attention. I do know that some thirty years later I started attending the First Unitarian Universalist Church in Providence, where the eloquent Reverend Tom Alberg presided. Once there, I noticed my future wife Debbie three rows in front of me. The next week it was two rows. The third week I was sitting right behind her. At the end of the service, Reverend Alberg asked everyone to turn around and greet the persons behind and in front of them. Debbie turned and said hello. We met at the end of the service. I asked if she wanted to go for a walk. She answered yes, but first she had to run off and see someone else. We went for the walk soon after, Debbie in a long green coat that was too long for her. I learned that she was recovering from a failed marriage. She learned that I was separated and mourning the breakup of my marriage. We were mutually charmed by Reverend Tom. He married us nine years later and just months before he died suddenly of a cruel illness. We were devastated and still lament our loss. The saga of our relationship will be picked up much later.

Years later, I proudly lead the separate funeral services for my mother and father from the pulpit of the modern version of the Underwood Memorial Baptist Church. I inherited no fewer than thirteen antique bibles from my dad, including one from the 1850s. I retained two for occasional display on my Hall of Fame bookshelf as a reminder of my heritage.

No one lived their Christian values better than my parents. I didn't buy into the church stuff very much even though I willingly attended Sunday school religiously up through high school. My father taught the adult Sunday school class. That said, I have the utmost interest and respect for the priceless sayings of Jesus, Buddha, Krishna and Lao Tzu.

I identify myself as a non-secular humanist and an atheist. We all have a conscience, or imbedded moral code, that lets us know what is right and what is wrong. In the end, what matters is not what one declares about their faith and beliefs, but how they relate to their fellow man. One of my favorite sayings is, "Whatever the question, love is the answer."

6
Wauwatosa: The Setting, Parenting, Schooling & Athletics

The setting is Wauwatosa; Wisconsin, Tosa for short. I cannot think of a cooler sounding name than Wauwatosa. My historian leanings led me to discover several interesting facts about the name's heritage. The first town meeting was held on April 5, 1842 and Charles Hart was selected chairman of the board. Until 1982, Wauwatosa was attached to the township of Milwaukee. Possible names for the new township created much discussion; the name "Wauwatosa" was suggested for two reasons: in the language of Potawatomi tribe, the word "wau-wau-tae-sie" means firefly: this part of the Menomonee River Valley housed swarms of fireflies in the summer and the name honored the Potawatomi chief, Chief Wauwautaesie. When the name was eventually adopted, however, the spelling became Wauwatosa due to a clerical error.

I am just going to state that Wauwatosa was an idyllic suburban village that met all of my childhood needs. And you have already read about its phenomenal Menomonee River Parkway and the memorable Hoyt Park.

In keeping with the idyllic community theme, I was blessed with idyllic, "salt of the earth" parents. Mom and Dad were gifted with an abundance of intelligence to go along with their high moral standards. Neither smoked, drank or cursed. Both began as teachers: my dad a graduate of University of Wisconsin and my mom a graduate of Eau Claire State Teachers College. In the summer, my dad's employment varied from house painting to a war time job at Allis Chalmers, working on the development of the atomic bomb. Their social life consisted of playing contract bridge with fellow teachers. With my dad's wide range of interests and expertise outside the home, my mom was outside the limelight in what seemed like a back seat. That was a damn shame, as her homemaking was every bit contributive to my maturation as was my father-son relationship.

My parents bought a lovely two story stone walled home at 1938 N. 86th St. in the late 1930's. The first floor had a living room, dining room, two bedrooms, kitchen and a bathroom. There was a finished bedroom on the second floor for Dale and me. Rumor had it that the Peacock boys would relieve themselves out the window when they felt mischievous or too lazy to descend down one flight of stairs. The rest of the floor was attic space, where two of my mom's nephews stayed during World War II. I would hide eight pagers and other pocket books with naughty contents in the rafters.

I was told that during World War the number two, my dad contemplated digging a bomb shelter in the backyard. However, a wiser head prevailed-my mom's-because a bomb shelter would offer scant protection in the event of a nuclear bomb.

There was a garage at the end of the driveway that paralleled our home. More often than not, a newish Pontiac could be seen in the driveway, as my dad had a strong preference for Pontiacs. I loved the styling of the Pontiacs as much as he did. When I reached my teens, my Dad put up a backboard and basket supported by two vertical poles about five feet into the back yard. It was a tremendous gift that kept on giving. However, there was a drawback, in that the basketball would all-too-frequently bounce over the fence and into the Beason sisters yard to the east. "Damn it", I would say to myself before tippy toeing all the away around their "nunnery" to retrieve the basketball. I have forgotten all the specific reactions the sisters displayed, but my recollection of their silent message was, "We are not pleased that you are intruding in our privacy." Right or wrong, I took on the feeling of being a naughty boy.

We had four concrete steps leading up to the front door of our house. Those steps would provide a compelling target. I would throw tennis balls at the steps by the hour. Sometimes I overshot and damaged the front door screen.

My dad, having been born on a farm and partial to flowers, went to work. Thus, our driveway and backyard were always full of plants and flowers purchased from the Burpees Spring Catalogue. Roses and creeping phlox lined the driveway and the east side of the garage.

Wisconsin was faced with the national polio epidemic of 1951. We were all quarantined and everyone had to stay on their own property all summer long. Unfortunately, classmate Bert Dyke contracted polio. Fortunately, it was a mild case of polio and he did not suffer any disfigurement.

When the family moved to Wauwatosa in 1936, my father became the science department at Wauwatosa High School and taught physics for the next twenty four years. His classes were so popular that girls began to take his class after hearing how interesting a teacher he was. He became famous for wearing a different Peacock tie every day. Many of his one hundred ties were gifts from students and friends from around the world. He also was known for taking his senior classes on a day trip train ride to the Museum of Science and Industry in Chicago.

In decent weather, my dad would walk the one mile to school, stopping half way at a bubbler, or water fountain if you prefer. Further on down, there was what was called a "haunted house", that was left empty from time to time. Then Liberace moved in and the property came to life with a fresh coat of paint and landscaping.

Wauwatosa had an excellent school system. At the time, I didn't appreciate what a marvelous educational opportunity we had in our bucolic, all-white and predominantly protestant suburb of Milwaukee, Wisconsin.

My education began in 1944 at Lincoln Grade School, with kindergarten followed by one through sixth grades. In first grade, I shot spit wads through a bendable plastic straw at our teacher, Ms. Liefer. When I'd hit her and she caught me, she would pull my ears until it hurt. Alternatively, my second and third grade teachers would send me to the principal when I needed discipline. This mischief-making was an omen of what lay ahead for my teachers.

My parents bought me an upright piano when I was nearly eleven. Isabell Dialy was my teacher. The first thing she taught me was the scales. When she thought I was doing my recommended practice sessions as assigned, she presented me with an adorable Stephen Foster statue. Foster was a prolific songwriter, known at the time as "the father of American music". After a year, my parents realized that I was not into playing the piano. RIP Isabell.

I've always said that my number one wish in the world was to be at a jovial event with friends who I had partied with for years and be able to sit down at the piano and start playing like Jerry Lee Lewis.

At an early age I found lawn jobs and went door to door after a snowstorm asking if the homemaker would like me to shovel their snow. It was hard work for a little tyke and perhaps said something about my willingness to do the work in pursuit of an objective.

My schooling continued next door at Longfellow Junior High for grades seven through nine. Wauwatosa High School was just across the street with an underground tunnel connecting the two schools.

A second junior high, Hawthorne, was two miles east, and distinguished itself by having the only indoor pool in the Wauwatosa School System. My father served as the Assistant Swimming Coach for several years.

I was a B student with a level A intelligence. That assessment is confirmed when you consider that I scored 154 in an IQ test taken in my junior year. While I inherited considerable brain power, too often I was insufficiently self-disciplined to take advantage of the many gifts I inherited. Or better said, if I had put the same amount of energy into my studies as I did into athletics, you would be reading about the eminent Dr. Wayne B. Peacock, PHD in some eccentric niche.

Barbara Becker was my only serious crush in high school. As she was a tennis player, we had the fun of playing mixed doubles together in a few tournaments. Our attachment lasted for a year until one day at the entrance to the tunnel going from the high school to the junior high school, she pulled off my ring from her finger and threw it at me without a word of explanation. I suffered a wound, but one that healed quickly.

I like to share the somewhat distasteful tale of my aptly named "spit split". My dad's Physics classroom was on the third floor. I would open the window and watch the world go by three stories below. There was a railing between the sidewalk and the grass. I would spit out the window and follow its flight down to the ground. Over time, I noticed a pattern that the spit usually split in two with one half of the wad going on the inside of the railing and the other on the outside. This observation led to a idea for how I could possibly win some money, say a quarter. I would invite Bill Schilling, who I sat next to, to join me at the window. I would innocently propose a bet that I could command my spit, on its way down, to split on two sides of the railing. Unfortunately, I do not remember how the bet turned out and neither does Bill. Oh, by the way, Bill would become the Class of '56's valedictorian and of course, I was not averse to catching a glimpse of his answers to test questions.

In my junior year, Dave Grant and Pat Hackney ran for Prom King and Queen. My fellow maker- of-mischief Jim Twet ran against them with Jane Godfrey, and Roger Fitzsimonds ran with Sue Torke. I was Jim's campaign manager. The candidates would drive past the high school in new convertibles, lent to them by car dealers, during the lunch hour. Jim was loaned a spiffy 1955 Chevy convertible, a model that has long since been lauded for its outstanding design. I would get carried away and drive so fast that the student audience hardly had time to see who was in the car. Jim would yell to little avail, "Wayne, slow down, slow down!"

One other Tosa memory that stands out is that of legendary Gilles Frozen Custard on Bluemound Road. It had been serving Frozen

Custard since 1938. By the way, both ice cream and Frozen Custard are made with milk, cream and sugar. The addition of pasteurized egg yolk turned ice cream into custard, and it was delicious, so Gillis was an extremely popular place for hanging out while satisfying one's sweet tooth.

Morning, noon and night, Gillis was everyone's gathering place. I had oodles of sundaes with three scoops of custard topped with marshmallow sauce, whipped cream and a cherry on top. Equally sumptuous were their malted milks. Then there were the delicious hot dogs I chomped down after adding lots of catsup. Anecdotally, the year Paul Gillis opened Gillis, he was in my father's physics class.

Athletics

Wauwatosa offered up a full array of opportunities for young athletes like me who craved the practices as much as the competitions. I took full advantage of the every opportunity I could squeeze into a twenty-four-hour day. I am justly proud of my achievements in the athletic arena as well as earning the reputation of being a good sport, team player and leader by example. A sampling of my favorite brags, achievements and stories I love to recall begin with the context of Wauwatosa being in the Suburban Conference, a high school activities association founded in 1924, with Waukesha, Cudahy, South Milwaukee, Shorewood, Whitefish Bay, West Allis Central and West Allis Hale.

Ping Pong

In my senior year, there was a ping pong tournament in the YMCA building across the street from the high school. I lost to Ricky Warner in the finals.

Tennis

I won four letters in tennis and led our team to both Suburban Conference and Wisconsin State Championships in my junior and senior years. I was the first one to have accomplished this fete. I was voted co-captain with Jim Darling in my senior year.

Basketball

I won two letters in basketball. However, being a sub and warming the bench for the majority of the games became my most painful sporting experience. I did not deserve to be on first team but I did deserve more playing time and an occasional expression of friendliness. One possible explanation for being limited was that Coach Walters may have had it in for me because of the bad blood between he and my father. Strangely, Coach Walters commited suicide a few years later when it went public that he had sired a black child.

Out of the blue, and for the purpose of shaking up the first team, Coach Walters started five of us reserves against West Allis Hale. I scored seven points in the first quarter. Let's see, seven times four would be a twenty eight point game with headlines. I was on a high, as you might imagine. Then he cruelly pulled us reserves off the floor and sat us on the bench for the rest of the game. Was the seven points in one quarter a harbinger of what might have been had I been given more playing time? For the rest of the game, I was left to commiserate with myself and the "what if" question.

On another occasion, I was subbing in a game against Shorewood High School when I spontaneously tripped Shorewoods' Gary Adelman as he ran by me. That was out of character for me. I was kicked out of the game, and rightfully so. I was sent to the end of the bench by Coach Walters.

Football

I won a letter in football while quarterbacking the team through a mediocre season. I also served as the punter and placekicker. Coach Pacetti was a wonderful man but not a great teaching coach. In my two years of varsity football, I didn't get the attention and quality of coaching I would have eaten up.

In my sophomore year of football, I put a cross-body block on my best friend, Alan Schmatzhagen. Alan came up with his knee into my kidneys. I was stunned but kept practicing. When practice was over, I went to pee and all I saw was red blood. I got a ride home after which an ambulance was fetched to carry me off to the hospital where I spent two days. That was it for my sophomore year of football.

There was an important lesson to be learned. While football players wear a kidney belt for protection, I did not wear my belt up high enough, thus exposing my kidneys to a direct hit. I was the victim of my own teenage carelessness, and I paid a painful price. Some things you don't get a do-over for, and this was one of them.

Cross Country

In my junior year of football, I injured my right arm in a Thursday practice. With the benefit of only one training run on Friday, I placed tenth in the Suburban Conference B-team cross country meet at

Estabrook Park in Whitefish Bay on Saturday. My time for the 2.2 mile course was 12:24.2 minutes. I felt very proud about the ease with which I switched sports.

Curling

Our four-man team won the Wisconsin State Curling Championship in my senior year. I was the lead and relative newbie to the sport of curling. The skip was my close friend Jim Twet and Dave Grant was the second. I took great pride in having done so while concurrently playing on the basketball team. To make it happen, I drove to the curling rink after supper to practice throwing forty four-pound rocks (curling stones] down the sheet (the frozen playing surface on which the game is played). While we represented Wauwatosa High School in the state championships, the sport was not sponsored by the school. The result was that we did not receive varsity letters for all our hyper-vigorous sweeping.

Cherished Story #1:

Out of the blue in May 1953, as I was finishing my freshman year, I received an offer from The Hill School in Pottstown, Pennsylvania. I had to complete a writing assignment in a Blue Book they had sent me. I thought, what the hell is a Blue Book? I tried Google Search, but was told that Google Search would not be released for forty five years.

I had some back and forth with my parents about the opportunity, but can't remember any depth of interest on my part. Apparently, my curiosity gene was asleep. I mean, how was a prepubescent freshman going to come up with the right questions? At the end of the day, I was reticent to uproot and move to an unknown faraway private school I knew nothing about.

The Hill School was founded in 1851 as "The Family Boarding School for Boys and Young Men." The "Hill" was the first boarding school in the United States where students and faculty lived together, under the same roof, in a family setting.

With the perspective of a reflective eighty-year-old, I regret not taking the drive out to Pennsylvania for a look-see. I can even stoop to the excuse that my dad should have suggested a visit before any decision was made. Maybe he did. Nowadays, any fifteen-year-old with an ounce of curiosity and an IQ of 100 would jump at the opportunity, even if he had to hitchhike. By the way, I started hitch hiking at thirteen-years-age. Of course, my brother Dale was the hitchhiking influencer.

If I had taken the leap and become a preppy, I wonder how different my life's projective would have been. I assume that a full-time tennis coach and a higher level of competition would have enhanced my development. Would the next step have been a tennis scholarship to an Ivy League school, or would I have returned to my roots and attended a Big Ten school closer to home? One thing is for sure, I certainly would have been forced to develop better studying habits.

Cherished Story #2

It was at the end of my senior year, when I was called into the Assistant Principal's office and confronted with, "You were seen drinking alcohol at the senior prom and therefore, you will not receive your varsity tennis letter." True, at the prom, I had gone out to my locker a few times for a swig of Gin or was it vodka?

Just who ratted on me, I will never know. The rumor was that it was Tom Patterson. The irony of the situation was that, not only was it the first time I ever had alcohol, but the prior week led our tennis team to a Wisconsin State High School Tennis Championship and had won the singles championship.

Cherished Story #3

During the 1956 graduation ceremonies, and to my surprise, I received the Lieutenant Robert Fischer World War II Hero Memorial Award for Outstanding Leadership. The presenter did not specify how I earned the award. I assume that being co-captain of our tennis team that won the conference and state championships for the second year in a row was a major consideration. That I quarterbacked the football team could also have been considered. My B plus grades may have contributed. And, that I was friends with nearly every one of my three hundred classmates says alot about my leadership.

All too soon, the majestic twenty-one-inch-high trophy was forgotten amongst four huge boxes of trophies. Those four unpacked boxes traveled from Wauwatosa to London, Boston, Cleveland before landing in the basement of our home in Rhode Island. It would have stayed packed away except that we had to downsize and downsize again when we moved out of a 3900-sq. ft. home into a 1200 sq. ft. apartment in 2017. Today, the trophy rests in a prominent position in my office, where it gets the reverence it deserves.

I've had an occasional bit of a guilt about not finding out what Robert Fischer did to become a war hero. In late 2016, as the universe would have it, I opened a box of my dad's newspaper clippings from the 1930's, only to discover Robert Fischer's photo in the top clipping in the opened box. There was Robert in his football uniform alongside the other members of the 1938 All Suburban Conference football team. Robert was the halfback for the team.

7

Hal Peck

Harold Arthur "Hal" Peck was born in Big Bend, Wisconsin, on April 17, 1947. He was educated in the one room schoolhouse where my dad taught all of the courses. He played seven seasons in the major leagues from 1943 to 1949 for the Brooklyn Dodgers, Philadelphia Athletics and Cleveland Indians. He reached the majors in spite of a shooting accident, where he lost two toes when trying to shoot rats on his farm.

In 1937, Peck's father-in-law arranged for a tryout with the Milwaukee Brewers of the American League. The Brewers signed Peck, and sent him to play for the Hopkinsville Hoppers of the Kentucky-Illinois-Tennessee League in 1938 and the Bloomington Bloomers of the Illinois-Indiana-Iowa League in 1939. He then joined Milwaukee for the 1940 season, and became recognized as a top prospect. Bill Veeck, the owner of the Brewers, identified Peck as his favorite player. Peck platooned in right right field for the Indians, and led the American League in pinch hits in 1948, as the Indians won the world series. Hal's lifetime batting average was 0.269, with 15 home runs and 112 RBIs.

In the summer 1948, my dad studied at Case Institute of Technology in Cleveland. The teacher and the student reconnected several times over the summer. At one such connection Hal gave my dad a ball signed by Indians Hall of Famers Bob Feller, Larry Doby, Lou Boudreau and Bob Lemon. My dad shellacked it and passed it on to me.

Hal died on April 13, 1995.

The Main Events: 1938-1970

8
Green Bay Packers

In the late forties, my romance with the Green Bay Packers from the NFL National Division League was birthed. Because I was born and raised in Wauwatosa, WI., I would be able to consummate the romance in person, with a comfortable one-hundred-mile-drive up to Green Bay.

In the meantime, I relied on the Milwaukee Journal and Milwaukee Sentinel newspapers plus Packer announcer, Ray Scott. It was 1947 and I was nine. Ray gave just the right amount of detail to keep me informed and connected. I loved his cryptic, just-the-facts-man style: "Starr, pass, Dowler, touchdown". None of the present day sports announcers come close to Ray Scott's presentation and descriptions.

The love fest with the Packers lasted twenty-four-years, until our family flew the coop to London, England, and never to return to my home state of Wisconsin. When we returned to the US eight years later, we landed in Rhode Island near the epicenter of the New England Patriots, Bill Belichick and Tom Brady. That might give you a hint about the future transfer of fan-man-ship from one team to another.

Story #1

In the good old days of my youth, the Packers played three games in Milwaukee. In the mid-fifties, I bought four season tickets. Jim Darling and I would occupy two of the seats and I would scalp the other two each game. Scalp, you ask?

Early in life, and with a well-developed history of testing boundaries, my brother Dale showed me how to scalp tickets. We would hitchhike or jump a train to Madison on a football Saturday. We'd proceed to a hotel lobby full up with excited fans, some of whom were pedaling their extra tix and others who badly needed some tix. Our game was to buy tickets at a low cost and resell at a higher price. While the profits weren't great, I had the sense of being in the savey crowd.

While we are talking about essential life skills, Dale taught me another invaluable skill; that of getting into football games without a ticket. It was simple. I waited for a family about to enter the stadium, then slipped in front of them. As I was passing the ticket taker, I'd turn a bit and point backward, while saying something like, "Dad's got the tickets'. I was long gone before the ticket taker realized the scam and he probably didn't care anyway. As soon as I was out the gate, I'd turn whatever I was wearing inside-out, and put on a cap, all the while striding along ever so pleased with my scam.

Story #2

On Dec. 31, 1967, Jim Darling and I attended the sports media had dubbed "The Ice Bowl" at Lambeau Field, in Green Bay. The sun was bright, but the game time temperature was - 20 F, with a wind chill of - 36 F. The field was treacherous because of the failed attempt to warm it up with in-ground heating.

In that iconic game, the Green Bay Packers faced the Dallas Cowboys for the 1967 National Football League Championship Game. Down four points and with time for only one more play, we watched Bart Starr score the winning touchdown on a one-yard sneak behind center Jim Ringo and right guard Jerry Kramer.

The Packers went on to lose the next week in the Super bowl.

Story #3

My wife, Deb, was and still is quite attracted to Brett Favre, the Packer's Hall of Fame QB. In 2006, Deb and I planned to attend the Packers-Patriots game in Green Bay with my son Daniel. At the last minute, I unilaterally dumped Deb for Ben, my oldest grandson. It proved to be one of my most tone deaf and inconsiderate decisions ever. I don't blame Deb for holding this brain fart of a transgression over my head to this day. I deserve it. As a repair bid, I bought Deb a Brett Favre statuette that graced our living room until it's head fell off. The cleaning lady did it. Ha ha.

Story #4

During the 2017 season Daniel, son Ben and I attended the Pats-Packer game in Lambeau Field. Ben's ear ached, so much so that we had to take him straight to a doctor back in Milwaukee. Morlean was alerted and she helped find a doctor that would see Ben on a Sunday evening.

Story #5

Super Bowl XXXI in New Orleans: Daniel and I traveled to New Orleans for the Patriots-Packers game. We took a big gamble, by buying our tickets from a tiny newspaper ad, i.e. they would have our check before we got the tickets. The hotel was in a sleazy part of town, as much of New Orleans is, which explained the 24/7-armed guards with heavy duty rifles.

Our seats in the Superdome were as high up, but seeable. In the third quarter, the Pats closed the gap to 27-21. I rushed to the urinal, so as not to miss the following kickoff. I heard a mighty roar. I got back just in time to watch the replay of Desmond Howards 99-yard return for a touchdown. The final score was 35-21. Our suffering returns whenever we think back on the game.

Story #6: We did a slow walk to the French Quarter while blocking out the deservedly jubilant Packer fans as they passed. I will never forget the stark difference of modes between the winners and us losers. The risque nature of the celebration, which included women baring their breasts, helped block off the glum, as did the beers.

9

First Racket, Tennis Results, Tony Trabert

It was happenstance that my father, Benjamin Noyes Peacock, moved from teaching all of the classes in a one room schoolhouse in Big Bend, to Wauwatosa and its high school as the science teacher in the mid-thirties. His salary was $1600 per year. Being the depression and supporting a family of three and then four, my dad sought out every odd job he could. He manned the cash register in the cafeteria at lunch time, announced the basketball games, assisted the swimming coach, and coached the tennis teams to several championships from 1936 on to his retirement.

In the summer of 1949, my father and now Wauwatosa High School tennis coach, put a tennis racket in my eleven-year-old hand at the Wilson Grade School tennis courts. Bingo! That simple fatherly act of sharing the sport of tennis with his son became the seed that grew into a tree of life and my identity for the following thirty years and beyond.

In 1949 I saw my first professional tennis matches in the Milwaukee Arena. Pancho Gonzales, my hero, Pancho Segura and Australians Frank Sedgman and Lew Hoad were the players I remember. Then, along came Tony Trabert, the most dominant male amateur in the 50s. He was everyone's favorite. My dad and I were also very fond of Maureen Connolly in the 50's.

At thirteen years of age and barely two years after I got my first tennis racket, I competed in my first competition. It was the Pewaukee Tennis Tournament. I won an adorable brass trophy for finishing runner-up in the fifteen and under Boys Singles. To this day, that slightly damaged sixty-six-year-old trophy serves as a vivid reminder of my very first competition.

What began as a coaching role eventually turned my father into an all purpose supporter and eventually fan. He, with my mother's aid, met every need a spirited youngster had, from rackets, balls, clothing, shoes to transportation, occasional suggestions and steadfast encouragement. Simply put, I could always count on my father and mother to have my back. My parents tolerated and overlooked the challenges my misbehaviors and occasional sassiness presented. I appreciated their care and attention, but I do not recall thanking them or letting them know how central their acts of kindness were to my pathway. Home, hearth, family and unconditional love was the foundation from which I had the opportunities to fly high and prosper.

When I was fourteen, I would grab my racket, a bag of tennis balls and jump on the No. 55 bus. I would say hello to Pat, the driver, and off he took me to the Wauwatosa Village. It was a short but peril-filled walk across the high-speed train tracks where both the Chicago and Northwestern Railway's Twin Cities 400 and the Twin Cities Hiawatha and Milwaukee Road ran. Both rail lines made the 400 mile trip from Chicago to Minneapolis. In addition to being loud, and sometimes scary, there is something majestic and other worldly about trains. Once safely across the tracks, eight hard courts awaited in City Park, where I would play the majority of my next six years of tennis for Tosa High.

Upon arrival at the courts, I'd warm up by hitting against the backboard on court #8. Next I would move to court three, where I'd practice three different serves: slice, flat (Cannonball) and American Twist, or Twist for short. If I had someone to throw up lobs, I would hit overhead smashes at target markers on both sides of the baseline and both the inside and outside corners of the service lines. After I was warmed up with my smashes, I would ask someone to throw up lobs and at the last second call out a number representing one of the four targets. This practice best represented playing conditions.

As I grew older, stronger and taller, my game improved and I won more awards. What had begun with a tennis racket being placed in my hand, had opened the door to a world of opportunity, competition and accomplishment. In retrospect, I had grasped every opportunity I came across.

In the fifties, there were only two tennis clubs in the whole of Wisconsin. The first was the high-end Town Club on the east side of Milwaukee. The second was the Washington Park Tennis Club with its two clay courts. Rolle and Marion Mueller were the pros there. Rollie provided my first and only professional coaching. By the time I was fifteen, Rolle told my dad that he had taught me all he had to offer. From there on out, I was self-taught.

My dad would call the Milwaukee Journal Sports Department to report the results of each match. When I was fourteen, I took over for my dad and proudly called in the results which typically began with my victory. Doing this reporting made me feel like a grown-up.

A few highlights and one low light from my career include:

- Ranking fifth in the United States at age of fifteen in the Boys Doubles;
- Winning the Wisconsin State High School Tennis Championship in both my junior and senior years;
- Playing against and losing to Rod Laver in the National Junior Boys Championships in 1956;

- Winning the 1956 Wisconsin Men's Open Championship as a seventeen-year old by beating the reigning champion and legend, Bobby Stuckert;
- Earning a full tennis scholarship to the University of Michigan;
- Winning some ninety singles and doubles championships over a fifty eight year career;
- Being indoctrinated into the inaugural Wauwatosa High School Athletic Hall of Fame in 2016, along with my dad.

Fortunately, my father and mother lived long enough to enjoy the fruits of their labor and behind the scenes support for my tennis career. I regret taking their support for granted and not expressing my appreciation enough for their selfless attendance to my financial and personal needs. Maybe I did? Unfortunately, for some things in life, there can be no do-overs.

A tale of eccentric creativity

In the semi-finals of the 1955 state high school tennis tournament, I injured my right shoulder such that I could not serve overhead in the next days finals. However, I did win the three-set match by serving underhand with a big slice that sharply curved the ball to the right and off the side of the court, making it a challenge to return with any speed and direction. I was able to call on this unorthodox serve because I had been playfully practicing it for a few years. There were three reasons behind my desire to have this eccentric serve in my arsonal. First, I had seen a pro using the underhand serve as a trick shot. Second, when the serve went in, it put the receiver on the defence immediately. Third, I was showing off so as to get attention.

Remember the Alamo

In 1955, I won the Junior's title in the Wisconsin Jaycee Tennis Championship. In addition to a tall trophy, I was sponsored to play in the 2nd Annual National Jaycee Junior and Boy's Tennis Championships at

San Antonio, Texas. The city is home to the Alamo, so I journeyed down there all by my lonesome sixteen-year-old self, without any fretting and stewing about my safety as my ingenuity and independence were givens in the Peacock household. My thirty-three-hour solo train rides there and back, turned out to be the longest rides in my life.

While there, I learned that in December 1835, during the Texas' war for independence from Mexico, a group of Texan volunteer soldiers occupied the Alamo, a former Franciscan mission located near the present-day city of San San Antonio. On February 23, 1836, a Mexican force numbering in the thousands and led by General Antonio Lopez de Santa began a siege of the fort. Though vastly outnumbered, the Alamo's 200 defenders commanded by James Bowie and William Travis, and including the famed frontiersman Davy Crockett, held out courageously for thirteen days before the Mexican invaders overpowered them. For Texans, the Battle of the Alamo became an enduring symbol of their heroic resistance to oppression and their struggle for independence, which they won later that year.

With the temperature well over 100 F, and without a cloud in the sky to block the sun, I lost to Donald Dell in the round of sixteen, 2-6, 6-3, 6-1. Winning a set off the top sixteen year old in the country was something I have savored. (Years later, Donald was inducted into the Tennis Hall of Fame in Newport, RI.) My doubles partner in San Antonio, Tim Frautschi and I lost in the Third Round to Robinson-Carter 62,6-2.

The tale of endurance

In 1956 I entered three events in the Rochester (MN) Open Tennis Tournament: singles, doubles and mixed doubles. On the final day of the tournament and with the temperature in the 90s, I began at eight am and finished my eighth match under the lights at eleven-thirty pm. It totaled twenty one sets in fifteen and a half hours of near continuous play. In the process, I won the singles, doubles and mixed doubles titles. My mixed doubles partner was Mugs Collopy and my doubles partner was John Inglehart.

The coming-of-age tale

In 1954, I headed south to Champaign, Ill. for the Westerns Junior Tennis Championships at the University of Illinois. It would be my first year in the Juniors. My escort was Bob Levis, who drove his dad's impressive new sedan. With my earlier years' experience in mind, I lead virgins Bob and Gary to a world of discovery and pleasure. The previous year, I had discovered what a whore house was and where one could be found. When a women answered the bell, I told her that I wanted to lose my virginity and could she give me a hand. My double entendre went right over her head. But I wasn't there to be acknowledged for my eccentric and occasionally off-color sense of humor. Her answer to my inquiry was positive and the fee was three dollars. She then asked if I was interested in an "Around the World" for an extra two dollars. I don't recall what went through my mind, other than if I went around the world, I might miss my next match. It turned out that my earlier year's trailblazing discovery of a means-to-mate without-a-date led to a bevy of Wauwatosa virginal lads making the pilgrimage from Wauwatosa to Danville, Kankakee and other red light towns. I've always thought that I deserve a statue somewhere in middle Illinois for my pioneering leadership.

The hitchhiking tale

We were hanging out in Kalamazoo after the US Junior Tennis Championships, when Joe Epkins remarked that the Canadian National Championships were being held in Ottawa, Canada in two days. With little cash and no easy way to get there, I said "l will go if you go". Joe threw his hat in the ring and off we headed for a Canadian adventure. After we had walked a few blocks, Joe asked, "How do we get there?" "We hitchhike," I replied.

So we set off on our 260 mile all-night journey. The first 205 miles went smoothly. Then progress came to a halt. We spent an hour with our thumbs out in the black of night. As dawn approached, a patrol car stopped and the policeman kindly agreed to drive us to the end of his territory. A few more short rides and we arrived at our destination with badly needed shut-eye.

I do not remember how I fared in singles, but evidence of our doubles experience has hung on one of my walls for sixty two years. We advanced to the doubles finals, where we were matched against none other than the number one No. 1 Junior on the planet, Australian Rod Laver, and a future teammate at the University of Michigan, Jerry Dubie. We were warming up and just about ready to start when the rains came tumbling down. No game, no set and no match. I had just lost another opportunity to lose to a future Hall of Famer. Rod went on to become the only player in the history of tennis to win the grand slam as both an amateur and professional.

Post collegiate days, I played number one singles on the Mckinley Park tennis team in the Milwaukee County Summer League. Later, I partnered with Ted Zimowitz, a two hundred sixty pound, six foot six inch behemoth in several doubles tournaments. It was the eccentric in me to choose a doubles partner, not by who was the best available, but rather who was most interesting.

I continued my tennis career for another fifty four years with varying levels of competitiveness. When my right shoulder became a painful hindrance to my serving and overhead shots, I called it quits, save for introducing Debbie to the game of tennis.

Trophies anyone?

In 2017, we prepared to move from our 3800 sq. ft. East Greenwich home into a fourteen-hundred-square-foot 1400 sq. ft. apartment complex. We faced the challenge of finding homes for the eighty three trophies stashed away in our basement. It took every bit of my resourcefulness and creativity to get the stash down to two smaller boxes in our garage. I was surprised to learn that the Salvation Army, Boys and Girls Clubs and other such prospects I called were not interested.

I came up with one ingenious idea. I had fifteen trophies engraved with the phrase, *Lifetime Friendship Award*. Then I presented the awards in person or by phone to several longtime friends as a tangible recognition of how much our friendship had meant to me. Twenty-five percent were lady friends of mine. When I presented the awards in person it was often a very touching occasion, not surprising since men do not express such feelings very often in our current society.

I lined up the next ten trophies to be engraved and drove them over to my engravers home. Sadly, when the wife of my engraver answered the door, she informed me that her husband had died. I searched for a new engraver without any luck, as they all wanted exorbitant amounts. Fair enough, their engraving was a business, when my engraver treated it as a hobby.

If any of you readers could use a free trophy or two, I have some just waiting to come alive on your mantle.

10
University of Michigan & Beta Theta Pi

I am wanted, and this time not by the police. In the summer of my junior year, I received a very enticing letter from an alumnus of Northwestern University who was a national level player. It was an invitation to visit with the tennis coach, talk about their scholarship offer and play some tennis with their vanguard of former champions. Impulsively, I dismissed the precious invitation with very little consideration or discussion with my dad. My dad made the difficult call to the school to say I wasn't interested.

I imagine that in my ignorance, I considered Northwestern a lesser school because their major sports teams were not so competitive in the Big Ten. Besides, I thought that Northwestern would not be far enough from home. With the wisdom of hindsight, I acknowledge how unworldly and shallow my decision making was. I threw away an opportunity with everything to learn and nothing to lose. What a day or two in Evanston, IL. could have been.

A capital offer: In my junior year of high school, the University of Wisconsin tennis coach began working on my dad to help entice me up to Madison. However, I had a strong bias against UW. I saw the program as second tier. Plus, I had a strong urge to leave the state.

As my senior year of high school was ending, my dad broached the subject of college: which one and what major. He asked the right questions, made occasional suggestions and, while he'd left it unsaid, it was clear that the final choices were mine to make. In life-coaching language, he was there to serve as a powerful yet quiet influence.

My dad went with me on a visit to Michigan and Michigan State. I don't recall much of anything on either trip. All I know is that I choose UM and its tennis scholarship worth $11,000 for room, board and books, plus a job peddling programs at football games. It proved to be a great choice.

Prior to leaving for Ann Arbor, my dad had asked if I had thought of what I wanted to study. Other than policeman, fireman or mailman, I had no clue about what the options were. My dad mused that since I handled math and physics with little trouble, I might want to consider engineering. Without knowing anything about engineering, I enrolled in the School of Engineering.

Once again, my dad had asked questions that made me think. He'd offered suggestions without any expectations. And, he had the moxie to recognize and honor my strong independent nature. Looking back, we were a great father-son team. He was the neutral influencer for my college selection process and choice of a major.

Michigan got their money's worth from my scholarship:

First Practice

About the second week on campus, Coach Murphy arranged for me to practice with Barry McKay, the best player on the team. We met at the Intramural Building with it's slick wooden floors, a surface I had never played on. It is very relevant because the ball hardly bonuses at all. It was a very pleasant experience.

An Upsetting Loss

I only lost one match In three years. That loss, at Ohio State University, was due to a severe hangover. When the match was scheduled to start, I was sound asleep on the ground next to the net post. Fellow team member, John Wylie, and I had gone bar hopping the previous night.

Several decades later, I found a clipping of the UM vs. OSU tennis match results in a scrap book my father had created. The first paragraph began, "Surprisingly, Wayne Peacock lost to so and so, 6-4, 6-1. Later, Wayne recovered by winning his doubles match 6-3, 6-4, with partner Scot Meantz."

Championships

I won every Big Ten Championship match I played in, which resulted in two singles titles and three doubles titles. Our team won the Big Ten Championships in 1959 and 1961.

Captain Wayne

I was voted Captain of the team in 1960 and then proceeded to flunk Spanish, which dropped my grade point average below the eligibility level of 2.0. Hence, I forfeited the experience of being the Captain of a Big Ten University team. In my fifth year of college and third year of eligibility, I was named Honorary Captain of the 1961 team.

The Arthur Ashe

In my junior year with the University of Michigan tennis team, I received a late Friday night call from Coach Murphy. He wanted me and two other members of the varsity team to show up at the tennis courts at nine am sharp the next day. We were going to practice with seventeen-year-old Arthur Ashe for a couple of hours. Art was the top high school tennis player in the country. Our job was to impress Arthur such that he would choose Michigan for his collegiate career. We played several sets over a two-hour period. We knew of his reputation but never would have guessed that he would become Wimbledon Champion and number one player in the world just a few years later. Had we the foresight to have our pictures taken with Art Ashe and his autograph, you would be seeing the proof of the story I am about to tell.

Near the end of our practice, I hit a hard, bullet-like serve to Arthur's forehand which he returned with even greater speed. I had been moving forward toward the net as his ball approached my lower mid-section. Without hesitation I instinctively jumped straight up in the air and returned the ball with my racket between my legs. And to top it off, the ball went like a bullet in the space between Arthur and his partner for a winner. Bam! Bam! Bam! Take that, Arthur! What is remarkable is that this was the first time I ever had this specific opportunity to try a between-the-legs trick shot return, and to a future Hall of Famer no less. Unfortunately, Arthur choose UCLA over Michigan. I like to think I might have scared him into thinking he would have to play second fiddle to me at number singles. Ha ha.

The next time I saw Arthur play was on my TV screen in Putney Heath, which borders the Wimbledon and Putney Heath Commons in London, England. It was July 5, 1975, in the first all American Wimbledon final since 1947. Ashe, just a few days short of his thirty-second birthday, and the number sixth seed, won the Wimbledon championship on his ninth attempt. He defeated the overwhelming favorite and defending champion, Jimmy Connors.

The summer of '57

In the summer of 1957, Coach Murphy hired me as an assistant tennis coach at the Town Club in Milwaukee. It was frequently quite hot and very sunny. I was bored much of the time. I would hit tennis balls with the ladies and offer a tip or two. I don't recall coaching any men. There was an exception to my boredom in that the number ten woman tennis player in the USA, Barbara Davidson, was a member. Playing with her was a privilege. We found ourselves to be pretty close to equals.

The summer of '58

In the summer of 1958 a Mr. Adelman, owner of a laundry company and father of Gary, a teenage tennis player, offered me a job loading and unloading laundry at one of his operations. A few months before, I got a call from him asking if I would practice with Gary on their private tennis court. I agreed without any thought of whether or not there was a compensation involved. Considering the meager pay at the laundry, bring an unpaid instructor for all those practices with Gary, and the incalculable thirty mile round trip drives to Mr.

Adelman's home, I had been had by a wealthy cheapskate. Grrrr. The life lesson I learned from that summer's experience is that I did not want to be using my musculature to make a living.

The summer of '59

I worked at a West Allis company manufacturing steel containers while living at home with my parents. Moving the 90 lb containers around the plant all day was heavy work and a man's job. My experience that that summer reinforced the life lesson from the previous two summers; I hate manual labor.

The summer of '60

I spent the summer of 1960 in Detroit working in Bob Quarnstrom's father's machining company. It was eight hours of hard work. I lived over a bar where I came face to face with extended loneliness for the first time my life. With nothing to occupy my spare time I read a lot of newspapers. The headlines were mostly about the Presidential election in November. John F. Kennedy was running against Richard Nixon. In November, Kennedy would win with 303 electoral votes to 219 for Richard Nixon. Harry Byrd was a third party candidate who garnered but 15 votes.

On the positive side, I played tennis a few times with a future UM teammate Ray Senkowski. A few years later we won the Big Ten number one doubles championship together which led to our team winning the championship. Starved for female companionship, Ray fixed me up with a Polish girl from his hometown of Hamtramck. How do I put this? I suddenly realized that I had been spoiled in Wauwatosa with its plethora of attractive girls. While she was a nice person, we had nothing in common, thus keeping our conversations alive was painful for both of us.

Looking ahead to national acclaim

In 2019 and 2021, our two Big Ten Championship tennis teams will be honored on Champions Weekend, both at Saturday morning ceremonies and at halftime of the homecoming football games. I will be joined by fellow Big Ten and NCAA champions in the other sports. It will be a thrill to come sprinting out of the tunnel at halftime in front of one-hundred-sixteen thousand fans plus millions more on TV. And to be joined by those of my fellow eighty-year-olde teammates who are still mobile. To see myself on the giant jumbo 85 x 134 ft. wide screens will be thrill.

Just between you and I

Psst! I graduated with the lowest possible grade point average. The 2.0 speaks for itself. Yet, and to my credit, I earned a Bachelor of Science in Mechanical Engineering from a top-rated engineering college.

Beta Theta Pi

Everyone spends their first year in a dormitory. I lived in the West Quad dorm with a roommate.

Each fall and spring, fraternities and sororities sponsor a sequence of social events for prospective members prior to the bidding and pledging. This is known as rushing. I rushed a few fraternities and got two bids. I pledged to the Beta Theta Pi fraternity during my first semester of dorm life.

Our pledge class attempted a childish prank but ended up pulling a boner and a criminal act. At Christmas time we went into a nearby forest searching for a lovely tree for our parlor. With difficulty, we cut down a thirty-foot-tall Eastern White Pine tree, or maybe it was a spruce? We dragged it through the streets to the House leaving a trail of needles to help the police find the criminals. How do you spell "stupid"? Saner heads took charge immediately by laying out the likely consequences: how about jail-time for the frat brats? By morning the tree was dismembered and scattered about distant landscapes. We held our fingers crossed for a few days.

Near the end of the semester my pledge class of seven went through Hell Week, at the end of which we were initiated as full members. Everyone gets a Beta name during the week. Mine was: "Peacock, the pornographic purveyor of putrid, pussy poking, pud pounding, Penguin penises." By today's standards, this is mild.

Beta Theta Pi is a North American social fraternity that was founded in 1939 at Miami University in Oxford, Ohio. The fraternity vision is that every member will live Beta Theta Pi's core values which include cultivation of intellect, responsible conduct, mutual assistance, integrity and trust. These are the underpinnings for their mission statement: "To develop men of principle for a principled life."

Early on in our first semester I learned that the elder fraternity brothers would go to the Pretzel Bell in downtown Ann Arbor to get inebriated. It was enticing but there was a problem of knowing I would be carded to prove I was twenty-one. Naturally, the thought that arose in my mind was that I would find a way to get around it.

When registration time came for the second semester, Jim Sexsmith and I got in the registration line, where I proceeded to write in Wayne Renford Jones as my name and a birth date threes year hence. After we had obtained our fake card and before paying for the card, we snuck out a back door.

I lived in the frat house two of my four remaining years. In the process I made several lifetime friends including a roommate, John Bloodgood. The fourth and fifth years I lived in apartments with one or two of Mike Browne, Bob Quarnstrom and Mike Brown.

The first concert I attended at the Hill Auditorium was the best. The Kingston Trio performed, and oh did I love them. I recently listened to one of their CD's in my car, sixty-one years after the concert.

Each year at the Hill Auditorium, there was a Fraternity Chorus Concert. We Betas had practiced diligently for three months when the time came to sing. We sang. When we returned to the frat house everyone's head was hanging low. Unbeknownst to me, we were off-key. A couple of brothers told me that I was he the only one on key. Who'd a known?

Each year we had a Mother's Weekend. My mom came to one of those weekends and I think she had a good time and was glad to have come. I have a picture of us in dance hold, facing the camera, which says so much about our unfamiliarity with dancing. As neither of us were dancers, we had no choice but to make the best of it.

Of our class pledge class of seven, only one other remains alive, and he is just holding on.

I am still in regular contact with Al Kaleen, John Bloodgood, Ron Piesecki, Jim Sexsmith and Bob McElwain who, not surprisingly, are all coping with significant health issues.

On May 29, 1959, in recognition of my leadership in campus activities, I was duly initiated by Vulcans, the Engineering Honorary Society. I have a certificate to show for it.

In the summer between my junior and senior years, Bob Quarnstrom was driving a bunch of us drinking mates around looking for action. We stopped at a bar and had some drinks. When it was time to go, I grabbed a bottle of liquor off the bar, put it under my jacket and walked off to the car. At some point we got stopped by a police car. The officer went around the car shining a light on all six of us. He saw that I was hiding something under my coat. He had discovered the bottle of whiskey I'd stolen from the bar. He delivered all six of us in the county jail where we spent the night. The next morning we were released without fanfare. The police had done us a service by getting us off the streets where nothing good can happen when alcohol is involved.

In the previous summer, Jim Twet and I were out cruising around in my shiny green Oldsmobile, I had purchased from Alan Schmatzhagens stepfather, Harold. The car had cool looking spotlights. We were preoccupied with the fantasies of healthy young boys that, somehow, two good looking girls would respond positively to our wishful flirting. As we passed a car with two prospects in it, I slowed down until we were close enough to flash our spotlights on their car. The car pulled over and stopped. The young woman driver lowered her window and asked what was going on. I made up some stupid reason for stopping their car. She informed me that her father was a policeman and would hear about this threatening prank.

Fast forward a year to the night I realized that I was not fit to drive so I pulled over to sleep it off on the way home from a bar. I was awakened by a knock on the car window by a police officer. He checked and found that I was wanted for a previous transgression, namely, harassing the young woman whose father was a police officer. He arrested me and took me, sans car, to the local jail where I had a great sleep. The next morning I was allowed to call my attorney. He came to court and told the judge that I was an upstanding citizen and a Big Ten tennis champion on top of it. His words did the trick. I paid a fine and was released to find my car, which I did eventually.

Swimming with a Shark: The Betas had a huge wooden cribbage board of some 24 inches. Cribbage became a favorite board game of mine. It was also a convenient excuse not to study for tests I had coming up. I was pretty good until one night I lost a ton of money to an older brother with no outward appearance of being a cribbage shark. His nickname was Gordy. Instead of cash, which I did not have, I took his meal job for two months.

I held down a meal job somewhere on campus seventy five percent my time in Ann Arbor. It is what I did, starting at the age of eleven. While principally at the Beta house, there were sororities and sandwich shops that always needed a handy dishwasher.

John Bloodgood had been Valedictorian at Whitefish Bay High School, a school in the Suburban High School League with my alma mater, Wauwatosa High School. In Ann Arbor, we were both enrolled in the School of Engineering, me in Mechanical and John in Electrical.

How stupid could I be? On the night before an exam for which I was not properly prepared, I got the hare-brained idea that we should somehow sneak into the office of the professor who would be giving the exam and take or make a copy. We proceeded to the ground level window and could see what might have been the test. I crawled in through the window and searched around for the exam without success and left the building empty-handed.

Friendship & Fidelity: Just as in the Army, when frat brothers hang out, hard hitting conversations, kidding, put-downs and laughter follows. I laughed more in the army and frat house than all the rest of my life combined. I am still using several of Beta witticisms.

As one might expect, I thrived on our intramural basketball, tag football and racquetball teams. And, not to be overlooked, the fraternity was the environment in which I took my first swigs of beer and coffee and then proceeded to make up for my alcohol free high school years.

When I returned from the Big Ten Tennis Championships at Northwestern University, having won the #3 singles title and #1 number one doubles title, there was a touching *Welcome Home Champ* banner across the front of the Beta House. Did I swell up with appreciation or what? It made me glad to be a Beta.

The missing link in my life, a steady girlfriend, created many conflicting emotions. As I figured out later, I was somewhat awkward and lacked confidence in my pursuit of the goal. Logically, one could assume that a guy with all the confidence in the world on the athletic stage, would translate that confidence into finding and developing relationships with women.

I recall one specific party in the basement of our frat house for which I may or may not have had a date. I was super jealous of all the cuddling going on in the shadows. I yearned to be in their shoes and, oh, just forget it.

By happenstance one afternoon, I met a gal who was as attracted to me as I was to her. She was not a student, but rather a resident of Ann Arbor. I invited her to our next dance and consummated our short lived relationship in the attic of the Beta House. Possibly due to the fact that we existed in separate worlds, it was the last time we would see each other.

Brother Al Killeen and I drove to New Orleans on our spring break. As we were driving into town, having given a young black dude a ride, a car pulled alongside with two angry white guys yelling at us while brandishing a gun. We were terrified to say the least as the last gun aimed at me was a squirt gun in seventh grade. We did nothing to add fuel to the fire. Eventually, they pulled ahead, our cars separated and, if I recall, we both had to change our underwear.

We arrived safely in the City of New Orleans, otherwise known as the Big Easy. My first remembrance was knocking on the door of a house of prostitution. When it turned out that the prostitute wanted more than the five dollars we could afford, we sadly walked away to drown our disappointments with a brew. How ironic that the woman to Al's right at the bar was a looker and quite likely a hooker. We behaved like the northern gentlemen we weren't.

11
Military Service

In 1962, I made what I believed would be a lifesaving decision. With the threat of being drafted into the US Army and facing combat in Vietnam with the prospect of an early death, I joined the US Army Reserves for a six-year stint. I must have figured that the odds were better in the reserves then in the Army. I will never know what might have been, but I do know that my reserve group was not called up and I escaped the horrors of combat.

My service included six months of basic training, followed by one night a week and one weekend a month plus a two-week camp every summer for six years. My attitude toward the reserves was best reflected in my paycheck. We started out as privates with the potential for regular promotions. My fellow reservists received three or four promotions in the six years. I, however, received one. I reckon my mental resistance to the loss of independence was all too apparent to my superiors. My resistance to being told what to do put me in a frame of mind that was antithetical to military service. Quit likely, it is about my power being taken away from me. I am not proud of my reaction, but I was what I was, an immature twenty-two-year-old making a quick transition from fraternity life to military life.

By far the biggest challenge for me was staying awake when we were only getting five or six hours a night during Basic Training. I'd go so far as to describe it as awful. Fast forward to fraternity life when staying up late to study for an exam was routine. It was awful there as well.

There came a breaking point along the "awful" road. I was so rundown and distraught that I made a vow to never be tired again. To keep that vow, whenever I felt heavy eyes coming along, I went to bed or laid down immediately. And, here is the solution only an eccentric like me would arrive at. I take off all of my clothes, just like

I always have done when I go to bed. This way, my system responds as if it was a normal bedtimes. Those lacking street smarts leave all their clothes on. Typically, my buck naked self would be asleep in less than three minutes. And one last thing; I leave all of my mind games on the burrow with my wallet, leaving me with an empty mind.

I went fifty years without realizing that I was a bonafide veteran who served his country honorably in time of war against the Vietnamese. When my military service was put in that context, everything changed. I sought out the dates when I could march with my fellow veterans. I began to seek out the opportunities to march with my fellow veterans in Memorial and Veterans Day parades.

There is one memory from basic training that has never left me. I was standing in the chow line when a black soldier and I caught each other's eyes. I recall recognizing his angry facial expression and realizing he had misinterpreted my glance. To this day I don't know what set him off or where he'd gotten the impression that I was looking down on him for being black. In a flash, he punched me in the face. Instinctively, I punched him back. We flayed at each other for a few moments, before our amateur fisticuffs were broken up by our fellow reserves. If there had been a referee, it would have been called a draw. Ever since that fight, I have taken immense pride in the defense I put up. The takeaway from this incident was my realization that I never wanted to encourage that sort of ire again, mistaken or otherwise.

Back breaking story: Beginning in my junior year of high school I felt a nagging pain in spine of my lower back. The pain was louder when I was resting because it was not competing with other noise. I figured my thousands of all-out tennis serves could have been the culprit or maybe the badly performed dive I took at the Milwaukee Athletic Club. I tolerated the constant discomfort for years as just one of those things I had to put up with. When I finally saw a doctor, he prescribed a corset. After six months of zero relief, I threw it away.

When I went for my army reserve's physical in 1962, I had hopes that my back condition would be evaluated and seen as a reason for rejecting me. That turned out to be a pipe dream. They were not interested in the least, so I had to get over myself. Looking back I've often wondered if my back condition should have disqualified me for military service. It is hard to say because it was so long ago, but I had always been physically active so when I was accepted, I simply applied that physicality to my duties in the reserves.

The constant discomfort in my back continued to be an issue until the early spring of 1971, when I could not tolerate it anymore. By then I had volunteered for an overseas assignment in London. Our family of four with one more on the way moved to Putney Heath, an adorable village just outside of London. My British doctor determined with x-rays that I had tiny fissures/cracks in my spine. Surgery was the only solution. What they did was take a metal file to the cracks in my spine. Then they took bone chips from my hip and laid them over the fissures. The chips quickly grew into the cracks, which thankfully ended the seven years of pain. At the time this was the procedure, a brutal one at that. Not long after, the doctors would be able to perform this type of surgery without breaking the skin.

A few hours later I returned to consciousness, of sorts. Thank god for the heavy sedation and pain killers. I awoke in a hospital ward in Roehampton, a quaint village adjacent to Putney Heath. It was my first experience of a ward, and I eventually came to appreciate the benefit of my prolonged stay. I was highly sedated for the first five days. My conversations with my parents, who had arrived from the states, must have been mostly incoherent. It must have been painful for them to be with their youngest son in such a helpless condition.

In the second five days I became more and more lucid and could tell that the cracked spine issue was resolved. The years of a low-level pain were over. At ten days I was released and from there on my recovery went exceptionally smooth. I returned to my athletic self again. Cheers!

12
Marriage and Children

The summer of 1961 marked a watershed. For the first time in my twenty-three-year old life, I was without the structure provided by the previous seventeen years of continuous schooling. I had no career, no girlfriend, and irregular and small paychecks. If it were not for my generous parents, I would have been less comfortable.

From time to time, I would find a mindless job laboring away but rebelled at the concept of using my brawn and not my brain. At the core of my collegiate mindset was the absence of a vision, a mountain to climb.

What kept me going was the satisfaction I received through my athletic endeavors. My tennis game was still there. I was playing in fifteen or more tennis tournaments each year, winning most, while also playing for the McKinley Park Tennis Team in the Public Parks League. I played fast pitch softball in the summer evenings and flag football in the fall.

I curled at the Wauwatosa Curling Club with three high school mates: Jim Twet, Dave Grant and Bob Roland. Together we won the Wisconsin State High School Curling Championship. In curling, your team is known as a rink. The rink is made up of four players: the lead, the second, the third, and the skip. It is related to shuffleboard. Two teams, take turns sliding heavy, polished granite stones, also called rocks, across the ice sheet towards the house, a circular target marked on the ice.

I enjoyed our inter-club league and as well as our intra-club bonspiels, i.e. curling tournaments. Tournaments are always the end game in the sporting world for me. In 1958, our rink, as teams were called, won the Wauwatosa Curling Club Championship Bonspiel, which elevated us into the top echelon of all men's rinks in Wisconsin, a feat we were justly proud of.

In the summer, I played catcher on Dale's fast-pitch softball team. There is a significance to me playing this position. In grade school, I would occasionally play catcher for Steve Daniels on our sixth grade team. Steve was the class tough guy and the best fastpitch pitcher in town. I was catching Steve's fastballs and considered myself a chicken, the nineteen forties word for scaredy-cat. Fast forward seven years to Dale's Village Inn team where I somehow found catching to be a position I could be totally in. Physiologically speaking, I was healing a wounded ego. Regardless, it was a personal triumph.

My other passions included golf, swimming, bumper pool, fastpitch softball, cribbage, and card games like poker and sheepshead.

The missing ingredient was a steady girlfriend with future possibilities. Then, by happenstance or whatever explanation makes sense, I crossed paths with a girl I had twice double-dated with in my senior year of high school. Our double daters were Mary Dahlke and John Iglehart. Her name was Morlean Mary Dowling. We had not laid eyes on each other for over six years. I had gone off to Ann Arbor to play tennis and consume, and occasionally over consume, two new beverages to my diet, coffee and beer. Morlean had finished high school and then college at the local University of Wisconsin-Milwaukee. Her first job was that of a teacher at the Mother of Perpetual Help School in Milwaukee. Along the way she had married and given birth to Christopher Thomas.

Whatever we talked about at our crossing-of-paths must have concluded with my invitation for her to stop by the ESSO service station I was managing in nearby West Allis. Nary a week had gone by when Morlean drove into my tiny and run down two pump gas station on a warm Sunday afternoon with the top down on her hip peacock blue Ford convertible. One-year-old Chris was strapped in a car seat. Wow, what a welcome sight to see Morlean as an adult and a mom. While I remember little of our conversation, I have long cherished the memory of our meeting. It would be too easy to pretend that it was love at first sight, I will settle for: It was a heartwarming re-connection." The feeling must have been mutual as it was not long before we were dating.

Morlean was attractive and a joy to converse with. It became apparent that our take on the basic elements of life were remarkably compatible. It was if our moral constitutions were sliced from the same cake. With each succeeding date it became more and more apparent that we were meant for each other. My many years of chasing after were over. I had found my soulmate. My life's trajectory was set and my world would never be the same.

Marriage seemed like the logical next step. Even though I had not gotten down on my knees, I did receive a positive "Yes" when I popped the question. Shame on me for not remembering the when, where and how I proposed. On May 22, 1965, in a service performed by our minister, John W. Cyrus, at the Milwaukee Unitarian Church, we tied the knot. The aforementioned Mary Dahlke was the bridesmaid and Martin Brooks, a friend from North Yorkshire, England, was the best man. Incidentally, I was twenty seven and Morlean was twenty five.

The night before the marriage we had a jubilant frat-party-like get-together for close friends and out-of-towners at Morlean's house. It was a hoot and had a homecoming-like atmosphere for my University of Michigan friends whom I had not seen since my college days, four years prior.

I had adopted Christopher prior to our marriage. The newly formed Peacock family of three soon settled in together at Morlean's cozy home in Whitefish Bay, WI.

For our hyper-modest honeymoon, we drove to the Holiday Inn Express on the edge of town for a one-night stay. It was a lame celebration, but I had to leave the next day on a business trip.

Our family expanded from three to four on September 5, 1968 with the birth of Leslie Anne Peacock at St. Michael Hospital, Milwaukee, WI. Before leaving the hospital, we decided to choose a name. I do not recall how we arrived at the names Leslie Anne. It was I who suggested an "e" at the end of Ann. I reasoned that it would honor that part of her later-to-be determined Northern European/English ancestry.

A couple years down the road, the phone rang in the middle of the night. Morlean's mom had died. In the moments that followed, I was an inconsiderate and disrespectful ass. I don't recall my exact words, but the tone was something like; "That is too bad, or I am sorry, now let's get back to sleep and we will go to the hospital in the morning." Wiser energy prevailed and we did leave for the hospital immediately."

At some point in time, I recognized that Leslie and I had always had a special connection, a special gift, as it were. When we would part after time together, Leslie's eyes would appear to be tearing up as she managed a fragile wave goodbye. It told me in bolded capital letters that I was loved and that she would miss me.

Leslie was athletic in the mold of her dad, which created lots of opportunities. She was strong and non-reactive like her dad. As the years passed and our experiences together kept adding up, such as skiing in the Alps or a golfing trip to Florida, the father-daughter relationship continued to blossom.

In the spring of 1969, an opportunity to transfer to our London office presented itself. I jumped on the opportunity. There was something about London and England that made it a walk-off home run. I could not have been more excited. We sold the house and our flashy new Pontiac. After touchdown at Heathrow, we stayed at the Cumberland Hotel across the street from Hyde Park, a national treasure if there ever was one. After staying in a hotel for two nights, we rented an apartment on Fulham Road. It was so cold that Leslie warmed up with her back to the open fireplace. After one of us noticed that the back of her coat had caught fire, we quickly snuffed it out.

Within a few days, we found a gorgeous complex of flats in Putney Heath. We purchased a ninety-nine-year lease on a six bedroom flat at Wildcroft Manor. The price for a ninety-nine year lease was twelve thousand, five hundred pounds. It took another fifth of that to make the necessary electrical adjustments for our appliances. At the time, Morlean was seven months pregnant and finding it very hard to move around. I was guilty of some not-so-funny teasing of her slow pace.

On June 14th, 1971, we were sitting at the kitchen table when Morlean announced that her water had broken. Not having a car, we called a London cabby to transport us to St. Elizabeth's Hospital in Wimbledon. In no time, our family grew to five with the birth of Daniel Benjamin Peacock. A wee few minutes after the birth and with Daniel lying unwashed on Morlean's stomach, there was a knock on the door and a lady came in and asked in her very British way if we were ready for our tea and biscuits. It was a delight and a keepsake moment.

The next day I gave Leslie a ride on the handlebars of a rickety old bike up Parkside A219 Road to see her new brother.

A highlight of Daniel's early days was the purchase of an adorable English pram. He never knew how fortunate he was to having been pushed through the peaceful beauty of Putney Heath and Wimbledon environs in that pram. We erred in not bringing the pram back home to the USA. If we had, and had taken good care of it, it is not inconceivable that it would have carried Madeleine Morlean, Leslie's first child.

Our kids experienced their education in Putney, Putney Heath, London, La Crosse, Cologne, East Greenwich, Madison, Columbus and Melbourne over their K-12 and college years. Their age difference should be kept in mind. Chris was seven years older than Leslie and ten years older than Daniel.

To my joy, Leslie and Daniel became athletes, a heredity factor passed down from a father whose very identity revolves around sport, competition and adventure. This creates a shared appreciation of the awe and wonderment available for those athletes who run road races and ski down Alp mountains together. To say nothing about attending a New England Patriot away game together.

In late 1978, Morlean and I went for a long walk in Wimbledon Commons. On the way home, she told me that she was seeing someone.

My heart stopped. To my relief, she was not seeing another man. My heart restarted. She was seeing a counselor as someone to share her sense of separateness. Being two thousand miles from home, raising three kids and having a husband who traveled weeks at a time, was not working for her. Who could blame her. The most likely missing link was my lack of presence around our home. My body was there but my mind was elsewhere and totally consumed with my job. There was a body, but no relationship.

Our audience got one person smaller when Chris left for Madison. When Leslie left for Madison in 1985, Daniel was alone with Morlean and me. Our environment would take a particularly heavy emotional toll on the quiet and reserved Daniel.

In the winter of Leslie's senior year, she asked if she could take a bus trip up north skiing. We said OK. I recall an Morlean saying, "Yes, go." On the day of the trip, I was driving her and her friend Shannon up Rte. 95 to the bus in Providence, when we found ourselves blocked in a traffic jam that was not moving. I looked at my watch and made a snap decision that the only way she could make it was for me to run to the bus and ask them to wait. I jumped out and started running down the middle of the three-lane highway, only to be verbally abused by a very angry police officer. I scooted over to the shoulder and continued running the remaining 3.7 miles to the waiting bus, non-stop, I might add. The cool and collected bus driver said he would have waited, which meant that my worries were in vain. Eventually traffic cleared, and Leslie drove my car to the bus.

Here is where things get interesting. The following day, a friend of Leslie's got drunk at an unsupervised afternoon party and then hit and killed a fourteen-year-old boy riding his bike. He was a well known up-and-coming tennis star. The incident made headlines. Ironically, the ski trip may well have saved Leslie from being a party to the accident that killed the boy. It was likely that Leslie would have attended the unsupervised party and possibly been a passenger in the car that killed the boy.

One day I came home and found that Morlean had moved to another bedroom. The following day and feeling rejected, I packed my bags, left a note and moved into the Wickford Motor Inn. Two days later, Leslie and Shannan surprised me with a Thanksgiving Day visit.

She wasn't going to leave her dad to spend a family holiday alone. That daughterly act of love and compassion resides in my heart. A few weeks later, I moved upscale into the Trafalgar Apartments on Post Road. It was a pleasant place that I called home for two years. Eventually, I bought a two bedroom condo further down on Post Road.

By happenstance, I stumbled across two teachers in this time frame, both with the same lesson. Once, when I was talking to Morlean's brother, Brian Dowling. While I was presenting the juicy evidence, Brian maintained a still and silent presence. His response, or lack of one, had a powerful impact on me that I will never forget. It took me quite a while to realize that he was not buying my victim story one bit. He was not colluding with me as so many others were doing. Years later, Byron Katie, my favorite woman in the New Age arena, said it best:"If you think the other person is to blame, you are crazy." She was wise, but I was slow to get it.

The second teacher I encountered was Ben Kleiber, Allendales Manager of Personnel, and a former minister. Just like with Brian, I presented all of the evidence. Ben listened intently, but gave no indication that he agreed with me. For the second time, I'd been confronted with my failure to recognize how blaming Morlean alone for our problems was unfair to her. Both Morlean and I shared the blame. The lesson I learned from Brian and Ben is that tearing someone down does not elevate yourself.

In 1987, Morlean filed for divorce. I found an attorney who stayed in contact with hers. I told my attorney that I wanted to offer an agreement that was fair for both of us. He told me it seldom works that way and I would be needlessly giving up any room for bargaining. I told him I was not looking for bargaining room. To arrive at what I would consider fair, I talked to numerous individuals. All of my supporters thought my proposed offer was fair and more than generous. Months later my proposal became the official settlement. My attorney told me he never thought my path to a fair deal would work like it did.

Several months after Morlean's filing and our separation, she called to say that she had changed her mind. But I was vindictive, and told her it was too late to reconcile. I had accepted her rejection of me, licked my wounds and moved on.

When we met for our court date, the judge acknowledged our proposed alimony agreement and then ordered us to go out to the cafeteria and divide up our remaining physical treasures and art work. Sitting across from each other in the café, we were scared to death, knowing on the one hand that we had found it too challenging to live together in peace, while in our hearts we still loved each other dearly.

To get the ball rolling, I gave Morlean a list of our things to split up. I proposed a process that makes things fair. Whoever wins the coin toss gets first pick. The other person would get the next two picks, then alternating two picks, and so forth. I think Morlean won the first pick.

Our divorce was final in 1989, twenty-five years after our marriage began. This was the low point in my life. If we truly weren't meant for each other, we would have been giving ourselves a gift. But we were meant for each other, and that is why it hurt so badly. Who knows what would have come about if we had been better equipped to express and communicate what was and wasn't working, and how it was impacting our relationship. We are taught reading, writing and arithmetic, but not a word about relationships. We saw a counselor together who was recommended to us, but she wasn't up to our challenge. Who knows what would have happened if we had found a highly competent counselor.

Three of my best friends, all women, provided an invaluable safe space throughout the painful and empty days of separation. They were Alice Schmatzhagen, Karen Quarnstrom and Elizabeth Browne, the wife and widow of my fellow Beta, Mike Browne. I owe them a world of thanks for standing by me during the low points of my life. Hugs and kisses in perpetuity for these pals.

Postscript: Daniel, Leslie, Morlean and I lived in the same house throughout the downfall of the marriage. The kids were in their early teens, an extremely vulnerable period of their life. They were undeserving witnesses to the infighting that was tearing away at their beloved parents. Even when they weren't present, a negative atmosphere prevailed. Throughout it all, Daniel and Leslie did not take sides nor join in the blame game. To their everlasting credit, that did not happen with Leslie or Daniel. Nothing could say more about their character and moral foundations than how they handled themselves throughout their worst nightmare.

In 1989, and for the following three years, I extended a written invitation to Daniel and Leslie to an all-expenses-paid week of skiing and companionship. Our first destination was Cervinia-Breuil, a tiny resort 13,000 ft. up in the Italian Alps. Leslie and her husband Jason had been residing there for several months. Jason was living large making pizzas and skiing. Leslie was nannying by taking charge of two kids, cooking and cleaning all day. It was a terrible experience for her. She doesn't have a whole lot of fond memories from that arch in her life.

Daniel was living in Columbus, OH. Leslie was living in Madison, WI and I was living in East Greenwich, RI.

We planned to meet at JFK and fly to Milan together. Unfortunately, Daniels plane from Dayton was delayed a day and he said he only had $40 on him. We told him that we would meet him in the center of town in Cervinia-Breuil the day later.

Our 747 at JFK was fully loaded but Leslie had not arrived. I was fretting out at the curb and telling the plane's stewardesses that if anyone could make it, Leslie would. Eventually, a taxi came screaming up, the back door opened and out hopped twenty- one year old Leslie with her suitcase in hand. We were rushed up the steps and into the plane, then down the aisle past annoyed passengers that all stared at us. Once in Milan, we took a bus and then a cab to our destination. Knowing that Daniel would have little money, we left forty dollars worth of Lira currency with the bus company for Daniel.

Leslie and I had a great day of skiing after a deep snowfall. When it was time for Daniel to arrive, we skied back down the mountain to the village. We stopped at what might have been a quarter mile up the hill. I will never forget the sight of this tiny figure standing all alone in the middle of the square. The next day we took the first car up to the top of the mountain. There was a tiny sign pointing to Switzerland. Down we skied to Zermatt, had a breakfast outside and looking up at the Matterhorn. Then up a mountain to right where we skied until lunch with the Matterhorn to our right and what a sight. We were having the vacation of a lifetime.

In subsequent years we skied in Park City, Utah, Taos, New Mexico and Keystone, Colorado. On day trips we skied at Breckenridge, Beaver Creek, Winter Park, Snowmass, Copper Mountain, Arapahoe and Vail.

Christopher:

While living in Putney Heath, in what would be called a suburb of London in the US, ten-year-old Christopher had to walk, take a bus and underground train before walking some more to get to The American School in London. I went with him the first day and he handled it alone thereafter. I liked that he was OK with going it alone. This turned out to be an early snapshot of a boy who would relish independence and responsibilities. It also speaks to the trust I had in Chris, and later Leslie and Daniel, to find their way in life without my being overprotective. Morlean thought that I was prone to take my underproectiveness too far, such as on the ski slopes and runs in Wimbledon Common, wherein I would return home before the kids. I can see how my ways could be interpreted as me not being concerned about their whereabouts and safety. To the point, I can recall one such instance in the French Alps when six-year-old Daniel was skiing knee deep in the snow, crying and possibly scared. It was relatively flat so he was not at risk, but done today, I would have skied right alongside of him.

Chris started out in the U of Wisconsin-La Crosse for a couple of years before spending his junior year in Cologne, West Germany. His curriculum was solely in German with a speaking, reading and writing curriculum solely in German. While Chris was there, and I in London, I treated him to a weekend in Prague, the capital of the Czech Republic. I picked Chris up at the Prague-Ruzyne Airport and off we went to a city bleak as hell, which had not had coat of paint since forever. Everything begged for a renewal project. Chris was all eyes and wonderment. We found out that Prague, nicknamed "The City of a Hundred Spires", is known for its Old Town and famous for the seven bridges that span the Vistula river. We visited a Czech Spa where my massage was 70 SKK or US$2. It is customary in those parts to sit in the hot tub after the massage and finish with a roll in the snow. While I took a pass on the snow roll, I know it would have felt great when the initial shock was over with.

Our time to play together provided a world class opportunity for each of us to release old and stale judgements and to make room for fresh new realities. We found out that we had much common.

Leslie Anne

I love getting a call from Leslie on Monday mornings when she is on her way to work in downtown Chicago. She is usually fresh and energized after getting some undisturbed sleep and a couple glasses of wine, not necessarily in that order. Leslie has been one of my teachers in that she will call me when I exceed a boundary.

In Leslie's senior year Morlean helped her fill out applications for Purdue and Wisconsin Universities. I pitched in by driving her on an investigative 2020 mile journey to Madison and back home to East Greenwich. When Leslie only spotted a couple bars around the Purdue campus, it did not impress the experienced high school consumer of alcoholic beverages. On the other hand, Madison is a street full of bars surrounded by a university, beautiful lakes and one of only four Capital buildings that is an exact replica of the nation's Capital in Washington, DC.

That fall of 1985, having barely recovered from the first journey, I once again got behind the wheel with a trunk full of belongings and Leslie by my side for the eleven-hundred-mile return drive to Madison and an apartment shared with another gal. It was later reported that on Leslie's first night in the upper bunk, the action in the lower bunk made sleeping a challenge. Go Badgers!

At the end of Leslie's sophomore year, her grades were not very good. She flew back to Madison and talked to her dean, who explained the level of grades she needed to attain. He pointed her to a high-level summer class which she applied herself to. She aced the class and received nearly all A's from that point on. Leslie was proud of her turn around and justly so.

Leslie attended the University of Salamanca, Spain, in the summer of her junior year. She returned with many fond memories. Attending DePaul in Chicago, Leslie achieved a Master's of Science in Applied Mathematics with a Concentration in Actuarial Science.

The next stop in her life was Burlingame, CA., for a ten-year stint teaching high school math at Burlingame High School. While there, she received her teaching degree and high school certification in secondary mathematics from San Francisco State University. She was emergency credentialed, so she could start immediately, as California was in a desperate need of math and science teachers. Her final stop became her home in Wheaton, IL.

Daniel Benjamin

I consider my communications with Daniel as essential nourishment. Our love is mutual. We thrive on exchanging opinions about athletes and teams.

He is an introvert and one of kind. He doesn't mince words and he doesn't waste words. His take on things is always fresh and well considered. Like his dad, he does not suffer fools gladly nor does he deal kindly with ignorance. He challenges my proclamations that miss the mark just as he would do with others. He employs the same courtesies with me as he does in his business communications. If he is going to be late, he sends me an alert.

I get a brief text nearly everyday and the most often the content concerns the sporting world or his kids activities.

I love every bit of him; his demeanor, his way of managing his own responsibilities and his way of relating to me as his father and friend. Daniel gives me a boost nearly everyday with a text or phone call. The usual topics are sports or the activities his kids are involved in. He always uses the fewest words needed to communicate his written messages, which is a great model for me and others.

Daniel played Pop Warner football from sixth to eighth grade and then town baseball in his freshman year. In the fall, he started playing both offence and defense on the freshman football team. His team lost in the state finals to Tollgate. He played football for two more years before concluding that the sport wasn't right for him.

In his freshman year, Daniel started as the number two guard on the team, and again in his sophomore year. He was out of basketball in his junior and senior years.

Dan played guard on the high school football team despite being undersized at five feet two inches and just 138 lbs. It said so much about his guts and determination. When, having played across the line from two hundred pounders, he would quite often come home with headaches.

I have a picture of him holding a javelin as a member of the track team. He placed an impressive fourth in the state freshman meet, then wisely opted out of the sport as a sophomore. His coach was negligent in allowing him to throw it as hard as he could, over and over, with no idea of what he was doing to his shoulder. Sadly, he struggles to throw overhand to this day.

One time in his younger days, Dan was swimming in the Wave Pool in Disney World when I noticed him struggling in the deep end. With my lifeguard entry, that I had learned a decade earlier in Hoyt Park, I tucked him under my arm and swam a short distance to the ladder. Morlean was justifiably scared stiff, before her eventual sigh of relief.

Like his dad and grandad, Dan wanted to go to a Big Ten school. Having been influenced by our time in Hudson, Ohio, Ohio State University met his requirements in spades. Over all, his years in Columbus were a huge success. Morlean and I got to celebrate his graduation with a lunch party.

Dan's first visit to Michigan Stadium, nicknamed "The Big House", with its capacity of 115,000 fans, occured when he was in junior high. We watched UM play MInnesota.

On my second visit to Ohio Stadium, also known as the Horseshoe and the Shoe, we watched the Buckeyes beat Penn State in the cold and rain. Thankfully, we had purchased a space heater for his room the day before.

On his second visit to Ann Arbor for the traditional rivalry game, the undefeated Buckeyes were upset behind an exceptional performance by UM running back Tshimanga (Tim) Biakabutuka. Daniel watched in silence and took the loss extremely hard. Most details have faded, yet a tiny scar may remain?

He spent his junior year at the University of Macquarie, in Sydney, Australia. As I wasn't going to miss out on all the fun while he was there, I flew into Sydney via a stopover in Hawaii. He met me at the airport and was anxious to show me around the sites and his favorite bars in the prison district. First thing he told me was that he had crashed up four taxi cabs before the police saved him from himself by taking away his driver's license. We drove a rented a car by the stunningly beautiful Sydney Opera House overlooking Sydney Harbour, crossed the famous Sydney Harbour Bridge on the other side of the Harbour and had a meal in the Rocks district. After the meal, we went for a swim at the very popular but hazardous Manly Beach. The beach is hazardous because of its riptides and exposures to dangerous fish.

Next we flew up to Cairns, considered the gateway to the Great Barrier Reef, in the tropical Far North Queensland. A frightful memory was a terrifying photo Daniel had sent of himself with an elastic band around his ankles on the top of a fifty 50 meter high bungee jump on Fraser island. He and his fellow exchange students had partied the night before and somewhat surprisingly, all the girls demanded that they could make their jumps first. Dan had no choice when it came time to decide whether he would jump or not.

Next we flew into Darwin in the Northern Territory. Then we drove three hours to Kakadu National Park and its 20,000 year old rock art. A river tour in the jungle was captivating in that the crocodiles were so plentiful, the fauna unique and flees unbearable. We did get to see that peacocks spend much of their time in the trees waiting to fly down and fights with a huge snakes.

After two nights in the jungle, we flew down from Darwin to Alice Springs on New Year's Day. From the airport, we drove by van 450 km to the Uluru or Ayers Rock Kata-Tjuta National Park Resort. Uluru is priceless. It is a justification, in and of itself, for visiting Australia in the first place.

Uluru is sacred to the indigenous Australians and is thought to have started forming around 550 million years ago. I did not realize the enormity of the monolith oval rock when we visited but now know that it rises 1,142 feet above the surrounding desert, is 2.2 miles long by 1.5 miles wide, with a circumference of 5.8 miles. The next day we climbed/raced to the top of the Rock. Daniel won the race in a breeze.

A fit young lady whipped my butt, but luckily I got to the top just in time to snap a world class profile photo of Daniel looking out over the sun rise amid the majestic views.

Our last, and equally incredible site, was a brand new national park, Kings Canyon. It had a smallish canyon with a waterfalls and pool. I remarked at the time, "Walt Disney could not have dreamed up something this delicious". It was a fitting final act of our father-son trip of a lifetime.

After a couple uninspiring and unchallenging jobs, Daniel found a home working in the Finance Department of Madison Square Gardens in NYC on March 23rd, 1998. At some point in Daniel's career there, it became obvious that an MBA would be essential to ladder climbing. A couple years of night school at Columbia did the trick. We attended the graduation ceremony with a great deal of pride. It wasn't because he finished with good grades but that he accomplished the deed while working fifty-plus-hour-weeks, commuting from New Jersey and still managing to be an attentive father and husband. It said a lot about his intelligence, capacity for managing change and unwavering focus on his career responsibilities.

13

Factory Mutual

The year was 1963. I had graduated from the University of Michigan in June 1961 with an engineering degree, and having never achieved a single A in any course. A year earlier, I had signed up with the US Army Reserves and had completed the six-month basic training. Now, for the first time in my life I was without any of the structures and security that schooling can provide. You could say that I was directionless, and lacking in general aim or purpose.

In this new and wide-open space, I was sustained by frequent tennis tournaments, fastpitch softball, flag football in the fall and curling in the winter at the Wauwatosa Curling Club. I remember a few dates, but no lasting relationships.

I lived with my parents but eventually started staying in Alan

Schmatzhagens basement for a spell. Later on, Bert Dyke and I shared an apartment in Whitefish Bay. I had a few menial jobs but none that came close to fulfillment. For the most part, I was supporting myself. I was happy enough. All that said, I was drifting without a plan. Then, out of the blue, a situation occurred that changed my life forever.

One idle day, I was with Jim Twet when he returned from the Milwaukee County Employment Office one afternoon. Jim, like me, had an engineering degree, yet neither of us was employed. Nor did we have a grasp on the steps to procuring a job. I asked him how it went. He replied that there was an interesting job available. The hitch, for him, was that he would be required to provide his own car for the considerable travel involved. For some reason, he did not want to pay for a suitable car.

Being curious, and one to sense an opportunity, I was at that employment office first thing the next morning. By three o'clock that same day, I was interviewing for the job of Trainee Loss Control Engineer with Bill Hickman, District Manager, at the Milwaukee office of Factory Mutual Engineering. I was hired on February 4th, 1964. My starting salary of $6,000 seemed fair, as I had no clue what a professional job like this was worth.

Our first training course was F&EC I, which stands for Fire & Extended Coverage. Some months later we had F&EC II. All classroom training was held at the home office of Factory Mutual in Norwood, MA.

Assistant District Manager, John Klovstad, trailed me on my first Regular Inspection at a small manufacturing plant in Fond du Lac, Wisconsin. After I had completed my inspection, we found a picnic table by a pool for John's feedback. I had done everything right by the book but there was one learning opportunity. The insured had six small heating units mounted near the ceiling. I diligently climbed up a ladder and checked to see if the safety controls met FM requirements. They did, but John explained that these units represented a miniscule risk. It was a memorable teaching moment.

After two months of trailing a senior field engineer on field inspections, I was making my own loss control inspections of industrial properties over six states and three Canadian Provinces, with some two, and even three-week trips. The purpose of my job was to identify unprotected property risks and influence the insured to eliminate and/or protect those risks. I did this in person at the property and through the loss prevention report I prepared for underwriters and customers.

Through my inspections and meeting with their management, I was selling loss prevention and control, which was the mission of the Factory Mutual System. In addition to inspections, Factory Mutual had written the standards for fire protection and conducted the leading-edge research on automatic sprinkler systems.

There was a lifetime of learning ahead and I took it one inspection at a time. My inspection reports would eventually reach the insurance company's underwriters and the insured. It was a job that demanded knowledge of how things work, what risks to expect for each occupancy, be it a paper mill or warehouse. The job required knowledge of our standards, perseverance, endurance, common sense, discernment and most important, vision. It was essential that one understood the core mission of our work and its value for the customers. High ethical standards were a must. And, a challenge that would ultimately separate the strong from the weak, was the courage and willingness to stand in the fire during inconvenient situations with the customer. Lastly, the ability to build positive relationships with the customer while gathering information and selling our recommendations, was a core competency.

I applied myself one hundred per cent to our loss prevention mission. It took five full years before I was confident that I was fully meeting the basic expectations of the job. Accordingly, my progress was recognized with increasingly larger pay raises and a promotion to Field Engineer in my third year. Incidentally, my six months' raise was a whopping $600; which pleased me very much.

For the following narrative to make the most sense, a description of the Factory Mutual System in 1964 will be helpful. The system was founded in 1835 by Zachariah Allen. In those times, New England was filled with woolen mills that were burning down right and left. When they did, they never got their business back because their clients would have switched to one of the other woolen mills. So Zach got smart and built his own mill with the best ideas he could come up with, on fire prevention and control. Then he sailed over to Lloyds of London and told them about the lower risk of his mill burning down, and because of that he thought his rates should be lowered. Lloyds pondered it overnight and in the morning told Zach they had decided that, "the good must pay for the bad". By the time he had sailed back to Rhode Island, he decided to start his own insurance company. Hence, the birth of Allendale Insurance. In the following years, as many as seventy other fire insurance companies opened for business. Fast forward to 1964, when the Factory Mutual System was made up of seven mutual property insurance companies, Allendale being one of them. The system included an Engineering Division, regional and district offices, a Research Division, a Test Center, an Approvals Division and the International Headquarters in London, England.

In 1968, four years into my career, our Factory Mutual International office in London was looking for volunteers to transfer to London for a two-year stint. Their field engineering needs were growing faster than they could hire and train engineers for a territory that included five continents. I went bonkers and had a response back in the mail the next day. To my great disappointment, though disappointment would be an understatement, the return letter said they were looking for engineers with five years of experience.

In 1970, a second memo looking for volunteers arrived to my delight. Having passed the "five years of experience requirement", I got an invitation and flew to London for three weeks of field inspections. I will never forget the visual experience of seeing London below as the plane made its descent into Heathrow Airport. Next thing I know, I am stepping out of a hackney carriage, otherwise known as a black cab, in front of our office on Victoria St.

To assure themselves that I was ready for international work, they assigned me field inspections in Southwest England, Wales, Holland, Germany, Portugal, Suriname in South America and finally Jamaica in the Caribbean. Their estimate of three weeks' work turned out to be five weeks of fourteen-hour days and seven days a week. It was an early indication of what lay ahead and my determination to get the job done.

The reports I submitted must have passed muster as in no time I was formally invited to join our international arm in London. In early February 1971, our family of four and growing arrived in London's Heathrow Airport. The dream had morphed into reality. The opportunity of a lifetime was about to begin.

From 1972-1978 I reported to Bob Kolbach. Bob was the perfect role model for the essence and practice of professional management. The examples Bob set and the lessons I learned from him have stayed with me throughout my management career. Many of the lessons were passed on to my direct reports. Bob Kolbach's influence was invaluable at a time when I was just getting my feet wet as a manager. The definition of man management, a term often used at the time, meant getting the right things done through others. That is what Bob did.

My first promotion was to a Senior Group Manager; then two years later to Manager of F&EC (Fire & Extended Coverage} and finally to Director of Engineering for my final four years in London. I created training modules, audit formats and operational procedures from scratch in our nascent international office.

Our first Engineering Meeting was especially memorable. We stayed in a hotel in southeastern France with a perfect view of the Alps and Mt. Blanc, the picturesque mountain that rises to 15,781 ft. (4,810m). On our noon break, we rode a tram halfway up for a once-in-a-lifetime glimpse around the alps and France to the north.

What had begun as a two-year overseas commitment evolved into an eight year once-in-a lifetime growth experience. From day one to this writing, I have been ever so grateful for the opportunity, and proud that I grasped it and ran with it all by my lonesome.

On October 20, 1977, a fire broke out of control at an auto parts storage warehouse in Cologne, West Germany. It was the largest industrial loss ever with estimates at $240,000,000. As the engineering boss in London, I dispatched Lutz Meyer, the local resident engineer, Ed Bayley, Senior Chemical Engineer and Ruud Bosman from London. The FM headquarters in Norwood sent an engineer from the Factory Mutual Research Corporation. A few days later I flew over to see with my own eyes. As I walked through the rubble, I picked up a broken sprinkler head and a piece of another broken head. These two relics rest on my Keepsake Hall of Fame shelf as a reminder of what the absence of high quality field engineering can lead to.

A loss such as this should not have happened because the warehouse had been protected with an automatic sprinkler system. Thus, the job of our loss control engineers was to find the answers. They learned that the sprinkler systems were designed to protect a moderate level of hazard in the 20-foot-high racks. What they discovered in the loss investigation was that over time, metal products had been replaced with plastic products, thus leaving the sprinkler system no match for the plastic. Regretfully, the engineers who had inspected it twice each year, did not pick up on the increase in hazard level. With Ruud Bosman writing up the loss for publication and my perfectionistic editing and additions, a powerful brochure was published.

When the position opened up I appointed a man named Al Hemond, who was a senior field engineer and assumed to be well trained. I had promoted Al to Operations Manager of the Paris office. It was my biggest personnel mistake. Not only because Al was a disgraceful failure, but that two worthy young engineers were bypassed. One story will tell all that is needed to assess Al's preparedness for his management position.

I told Al I wanted to trail him, so he took me to a warehouse location he had recently inspected. As he had made a recommendation for automatic sprinklers in a 5000 sq. ft. area of the building, it was logical that I have a peek. I looked at the contents of the area and found it was 100% metal, meaning sprinklers were not needed. I looked to him and asked him to explain. He couldn't. Come to find out he had made up the recommendation after he had left the plant. Al turned out to be incompetent, fraudulent and undeserving of his credentials. He was replaced immediately, and sent back to Montreal, Canada. I confirmed the incident for his personnel file.

The lesson I validated here is the value and necessity of the Russian proverb Doveryai, "Trust, but verify". In Factory Mutual terminology, spot trailing field engineers and other underlings should be near the top of executive management's accountabilities as a supplement to report review and field audits. And besides, getting out from behind a desk and into the fray, is so, so refreshing.

In early June 1979, we sailed the Atlantic on the QE2 from Southampton to New York, taking 4 days 16 hours. It was a voyage of a lifetime for our family. One day I played in a bridge tournament which was a rare but fun happening. The next day Morlean and I gathered in a semi-circle out on the deck to have a casual conversation with 29-year-old Meryl Streep, curled up under a warm blanket outside on a deck chair.

The last movie Morlean and I saw before returning to the states was "The Deer Hunter" starring Meryl Streep and Robert De Niro. It went on to win the Academy Award for Best Picture and it marked Meryl Streep's first Academy Award Nomination for Best Supporting Actress. She had me at "Hi", and has been my favorite actress for the 39 years hence. Along the way, she has been acclaimed as the best actress of her times for Out of Africa.

What a treat to be in her presence knowing that we were witnessing an incredibly gifted actress. I didn't know it at the time, but she happened to be pregnant with her son, Henry Gummer.

Three weeks after arriving in the Norwood, MA area, Morlean found a lovely colonial home she liked. I came home from work, walked in the front door and out the back door, looked around the yard, and said, "let's get it." The asking price was $99,000. The real estate person shared that an interested couple were flying in from the west coast the next day. The traditional approach would have been to offer five per cent less than asking price and negotiate. I reckoned that this situation was an exception and that we should not take any chances of losing it. So we bought it at the asking price. Two days after we moved in the well went dry. The probable reason was that Leslie was using two or three towels a day, while the current home owners were using two a week. We notified the seller. He felt terrible and said he would pay for the drilling of a new well. This is an example of how important it is to deal with those who emit integrity.

One day I came home from work to be greeted by an American Cocker Spaniel puppy. My family had purchased Taffy at a local shop. My perception of Cocker Spaniels was that of cuddly lap dogs meant for girls. Oh was I wrong, and happily so. I learned that Cocker Spaniels are tough as they come. Over the course of the next year, Taffy went from following me to the edge of our yard, to staying right with me on twenty-mile pre-marathon training runs. Before I began the twenty-milers, I would drive out to the ten-mile turnaround and leave plenty of water for my cherished pal.

Upon returning to the United States, I was assigned to Factory Mutual's home office in Norwood with a desk in the basement, no less. It was an ego deflator, considering my four years of trailblazing senior management accountabilities and successes in London. I was given three meaningless assignments during my time in the basement. Rather than choosing to feel under appreciated, I saw an opportunity for greatly expanding Factory Mutuals current distribution of loss information. I came up with the concept of collectively studying large property loses in search of invaluable lessons. I named it Learning from Losses. I enlisted John Klovstad, a fellow home office engineer of great intelligence and experience as my partner.

We would identify a specific loss, schedule a workshop in the relevant district office, identify those field engineers and research scientists who had a horse in the race, conduct the workshop and distribute what I termed a ge Lessons Learned summary throughout the organization. It is an understatement to say that the participants came to a fuller appreciation of our loss prevention principles after having dissected losses like never before.

John and I determined which losses were preventable and which were not. Low and behold, we found that fifty of fifty nine losses were preventable. While it was not a big surprise to us, our wish was that it would catch the attention of the Factory Mutual Systems executives. Sadly, this was not the case.

I was at my basement desk in Norwood when I received a call from Jack Carey, President of Allendale Insurance in Johnston, RI. I was offered the job of Vice President of Staff Engineering; a huge opportunity for growth and advancement. The only condition was that I would first have to spend two years as Engineering Manager in Allendale's regional office in Cleveland, as they were going to terminate the current Account Engineering Manager. I was flattered and overjoyed. We were on the move again. We sold our home for

$120,000, a nifty twenty percent gain in a single year, and moved into a home in the historically charming town of Hudson, Ohio.

There is a background story to Mr. Carey's invitation. A few years prior, I was Director of Engineering at Factory Mutual International (FMI) in London at the same time as Jack, the number two man at Arkwright Boston, who was sent over to FMI to be Managing Director. We soon became friends and fellow expatriates. Apparently, Jack saw a leadership gene in me. Stay tuned.

A year or so later, Jack got promoted to chief executive officer at Arkwright-Boston Insurance. Not long after, Arkwright-Boston held an Engineering Conference at the Chatham Bars Inn on the cape in Massachusetts. Jack invited me to be the guest speaker for the conference. I gladly accepted and flew over from London to party and golf with the Arkwright account engineers. The first night we played poker together. I was imbibing so much that it came to a point where Jack had to wake me to tell me I had won the pot.

14
Allendale Insurance

Upon arrival in Cleveland Morlean and the kids and I stayed in a hotel while looking for a place to live. We heard very good things about Hudson, so we headed south-east. As we entered town, we stopped for a red light, and we immediately felt charmed by what we saw. We drove through a historic district that was surrounded by lovely homes. Within a minute of entering Hudson, Morlean said, "I want to live here." We found a delightful home and moved in a month later, only to find that when it rained, water leaked into the basement. The problem was that French drains were not installed around the house. Guess who had to pay to have them installed.

Managing Allendale Insurance Company account engineers, as opposed to Factory Mutual field engineers, was a seamless transition. My biggest accomplishments were trimming the staff from fourteen to ten and preparing Greg Huigens to be my replacement.

To my delight, the VP-Staff Engineering job with Allendale Insurance, opened a year earlier than predicted. For the third time in three years, we picked up and moved everything to East Greenwich, Rhode Island. The family responded very well when they were told about our impending move. The same goes for the previous two moves.

Our home search did not last long. We found a four-bedroom colonial home on a cul-de-sac in East Greenwich. Leslie and Daniel had a ten minute walk to their East Greenwich High School.

We were happy with the house, but after the first week an issue arose in the backyard, it smelled of human sewage. We found that the underground system was undersized and there may have been too much clay. We had to increase the capacity.

It was discouraging that all three of the lovely colonial properties had hidden flaws that were not identified by the guys we paid one hundred dollars to find.

In the front of the school was a five-foot-deep well that was home for trash and food scraps. Taffy would jog the ten minute distance, descend into the well, eat every bit of food and paper that smelled like food and then bark, and bark some more. Eventually, Leslie would be called down to the principal's office where she would be dispatched to take care of her mischievous pet. This pet story gets better, or worse, depending on how your mind processes the reality that dogs go number two. In the winter, Taffy would chew on frozen dog turds. One of us would call, "No Taffy", or "No Taffy, don't eat that turd."

Not long after we arrived, I invited four Beta Theta Pi brothers to come up and reminisce about the good old days. They were Bob Quarnstrom, Bob McElwain, Mike Browne and John Feledy. Mike arrived early. He drank most of the night with my brother and got annoyingly inebriated. Entertaining him for a day was excruciatingly difficult because he was such a good friend and we had spent many hours having fun and adventure together, but never anything like this. It was a circumstance I never want to be in again.

In the late seventies, my parents moved out of their suburban home in Brookfield and into a small apartment complex designed for elders. Things went smoothly until my mom lost her fight with Alzheimer's disease. For the rest of her seven years of life she lay comatose. I learned about her death while lying in a late night pile of twenty-four mates who were on a camping trip in Colorado. Someone tapped me on my shoulder and whispered that my mother had died. The next day I took a cab and a bus back to the Denver International Airport, from which, I flew back to Milwaukee.

On the flights back home I made out a list of who to contact, created a program for her service, contacted the pastor, set things up for the wake and funeral service.

I called Daniel and asked him to bring my boom box and the Judy Collins CD with Amazing Grace on it. That song, sung by Judy and almost anyone else, touches me like no other.

I miss my mom. She was a fabulous woman in every respect, yet took the back seat to my widely well known father. My regrets center around not having spent anywhere near enough time with her. She would have been a perfect buddy for me if the two of us had created that heart to heart connection.

During our time in East Greenwich, one day I received a call from my dad, eighty- nine-year old at the time. in Hawaii. His voice was barely audible. He asked if I would fly out and escort him home because he was so weak that the hospital would not release him without an escort. I said I would be out there as soon as I could get a flight. Recognizing his deteriorating health, he had planned his trip to Hawaii to be his last.

Two days later I arrived in Kahului Airport in Maui after a long day of flying. I went straight to the nearest high school track and stretched out my legs with five mile run. Not long after, I greeted my dad at the nearby hospital. He was extremely relieved and even managed some smiles. I told him that since I flew all that way, I was not leaving without getting a good sense of Maui and its sights. For the next three days I went full out in vacation mind after spending breakfast and dinner with Dad. Riding a rented bike down from the 10,023 foot summit of Haleakala Crater is a hoot. Haleakala dominates the island. Other highlights were include Lahaina, a cute little coastal village and Wailua Falls.

When it came time to leave, I escorted him slowly to the car, but twice before we reached the car, his legs collapsed and I had to support and steady. The flights back to Milwaukee and his nursing home were uneventful.

This touching father and son love story was a most poignant reminder of the passing of time. It took great courage and positivity for my dad to undertake a trip this challenging. It says that he was determined to play the game of life through to the final whistle, regardless of the risks. Finally, it gave me a chance to pay back a tiny portion of what he had given me.

Less than two years later, my father, Benjamin Noyes Peacock died of heart failure at the age of 91. His heart just stopped pumping. His ashes lay in rest at the Schmidt & Bartelt Funeral Home in Wauwatosa. I lead the funeral services at the Underwood Memorial Baptist Church including the Willie Nelson version of Amazing Grace. He was buried alongside his parents, his wife Florence and Dale in the family plot he had purchased in his birth home village of Big Bend. Following the service, Leslie and I went to the home on my dad's childhood farm, knocked on the door and asked the lady if she minded if we scattered some of my father's ashes in the surrounding farm. After she took a deep swallow, she confided in her husband and said it would be OK. We each portioned out a handful of dried bone fragments, which are frequently erroneously called ashes, and threw them into the corn stocks. It was the first time either of us had held human remains. Our act reminded me of the phrase, "Dust thou art, and unto to dust shalt return". This phrase has its origins in Genesis 3:19 from the King James Version of the Bible and the meaning of which is: after death our bodies revert to their earthly, elemental components.

Having been offered the title of VP of Staff Engineering two years earlier, it was a good feeling when I finally assumed the position. I was now accountable for job descriptions, account engineering training and regional audits. I had line management accountabilities for my staff engineers and secretaries. I had a personal secretary, Judy Dassuncao, who would become a lifelong friend.

It was cool to be on the Management Committee and the engineering spokesperson for a global company. By the end of my first year, I was promoted to Senior Vice President-Staff Engineering, a position I held until early retirement at the end the twentieth century. I was handed the platform from which to develop all aspects of account engineering. This eventually became a story of how one man had the savvy and perseverance to spread the gospel of property loss prevention across five continents and twenty-three countries.

At the dinner following my first management meeting, I spoke about what I saw as the purpose and mission of account engineering. It was my first opportunity to communicate with colorful visuals, something no one else was doing. I made a powerful first impression on the executives. Other colleagues mentioned my refreshing optimism about the possibilities that lay ahead.

My proudest contribution to Allendale was my development of the Allendale Loss Expectancy Control" program, ALEC., was my with the greatest fiscal benefits.

My concept sprange out of a 1961 Senior Management Meeting, where in George West, the best executive leader II have every had the privilege of working under, sited Allendale's latest combined loss and expense ratio was 136%. He added that we were experiencing two $10,000,000 losses each year. That would be two losses of $85,000,000 in 2018 dollars. I spoke up to the top dog to say that, "I can take care of that", meaning the large losses. Having never heard something like that in the boardroom, he asked how I was going to do that. Without hesitation, I replied "I did not know but that I would figure it out promptly." He asked me to work with Charlie Anderson, the third highest executive. In a matter of days, I figured it out and shared my plan with Charlie:

The What: That we concentrate our resources on the locations most likely to experience a $10,000,000 loss.

The How: That we ask Allendale account engineers to pass on the names of locations that they think warrant special attention.

That we ask every FM/FMI offices to identify the 250 high risk locations that they are most concerned about.

That we ask FM/FMI offices to assign their most competent and experienced engineers to the high risk locations and to work hand in hand with the account engineer when joint visits would be a wise move.

With the help of Jack Powers and Dick Morley, we introduced the ALEC program to Allendale offices across the globe. Because of my love for travel, I assigned myself to the London, Paris and Melbourne offices. My Melbourne trip was quite eventful, to say the least. When I arrived in Melbourne, I checked into the nearby Marriott Hotel straight away. Next, I proceeded to do what I always do in circumstances such as this. I donned my running gear and took off on a long run at a nearby park. I finished my run and began my cool down walk. While doing so, I got inspired to run one more lap around the park. Half way done, I tripped on the gravel path and landed on my face, chest and hands. I was stunned and traumatized, but remained conscious. I managed to get back to the desk at the

Marriott where a desk clerk took one look at me and called a doctor. The doctor who came to my room and began the process of removing all of the gravel from my face, chest and hands, bandaged me up from head to waist. My hands looked like I was wearing white boxing gloves. Much of my face was covered. I had broken several small bones in the top of my right hand. The doctor gave me the choice of operating or not. I chose not to operate and that decision turned out to be a smart one, as my hands eventually healed completely without any bandaging.

Later that afternoon, I returned to the front desk to make a purchase. When it came time to pay, my boxing glove sized bandages impeded entry to my pocket. So I invited the lady to reach into my pocket and extract the amount needed. She was business-like in going about the retrieving of my wallet, a task unlikely to be found in her job description. With my dreams and aspirations for the trip crushed, I remembered a favorite buddhist saying of mine—Given what is, what's next?

I had brought along my golf clubs for a round of golf with Art Miltons, a fellow Factory Mutual engineer, who belonged to the Victoria Golf Club, a highly rated course in Australia. I had further plans to golf in Singapore, Malaysia, including heavenly Tioman Island, off the east coast. To not be able to play golf after lugging around forty pounds of clubs more than ten thousand miles, was a downer.

The next day I led the ALEC workshop. In spite of a heavy dose of painkillers, my discomfort and fever was readily obvious to the class. At the end of the training day, as class was being dismissed, Jack Woods, the Regional Engineering Manager, offered high praise for my courage in carrying through with the workshop, having suffered through so much. That afternoon on my way back to the hotel, I got the urge to see if I could retrieve my front tooth. Sure enough, I found it right where I had tripped.

My training tour's next stop was Singapore, where I awkwardly conducted the ALEC workshop as planned. As I am always want to do, I asked Mui Hua, the Office Manager, where I could get a good massage. She spoke highly of the famous blind masseur, Teo Seng Huat, who had his Galaxy De Sauna in the basement of the Concorde

Hotel next door. He was renowned for his foot reflexology, Taiwanese style shiatsu, Japanese style massage and Swedish oil massage. He worked on the floor and with a parallel rope overhead that he held onto when he walked on my back. I kept his keepsake business card as a momento. He was that unique. The next day my flight home began with a supersonic SST Concorde flight to Copenhagen. The round windows in the SST were extremely tiny, making gazing very difficult. In my brief tour of Copenhagen I visited the Little Mermaid, a beautiful bronze statue displayed on a rock at Langelinje Pier. I took a quick flight to London where I was so happy to be with my family and own bed again.

The ALEC program training was completed throughout the world one year after its introduction. The results were astonishing. Over the following two years, Allendale Insurance did not experience a single loss over $10,000,000, and our bottom line went from deep red to solid black for the first time in years. An "atta boy" from the front office would have meant a lot. I do not recall any formal recognition for the millions of dollars Allendale benefitted by from this innovative program. With that in mind, picture me taking a deep bow of gratitude for the opportunity to actualize my creative genes on one of life's stages.

I was born with a "Do the Right Things Right" gene. And I'd add, "to the best of my ability." Of all my genes, my Quality First gene may have served me best. As my interest in Quality Improvement began to bloom, I did what I always seek to do. That is, to sit at the feet of the originator/leader/number one spokesman on the topic. In this case, I was attending one of Phillip B. Crosby's workshops. I was enthralled with his message. My next step, was to schedule Phillip as the keynote speaker at our upcoming Engineering Conference in Coral Gables, FL. His presentation made a significant impact on our top brass. As a result, a Quality Improvement Committee was created, with Carol Peterson as the Chairman and I as an enthusiastic member. My first contribution was to create the following corporate policy statement:

Allendale Insurance - Policy Statement on Quality

We are committed to customer satisfaction through the timely delivery of quality products and services. We define quality as meeting customer and job requirements. We will do things right the first time through an attitude of prevention. We will measure the results of our work and make continuous improvements to meet requirements of our customers and associates."

More than anyone in the FM System, I used creative audio visuals, designed almost exclusively by John Young and his staff in the Audio Visuals department. God bless him for his support. I hope to get in contact with him again.

In 1998, my boss and Allendale's President, Charlie Anderson, brought me into his office and informed me that executive management was not pleased with my performance and as a result I was now on probation. I was given papers outlining the rationale and the areas that I needed to improve and a week by week outline on how I was going to go about making the improvements. I did so in a true Peacock fashion, by accepting his assessment of my work, followed by the best efforts I could muster. My next Monthly Report was replete with purposeful and responsive data and information.

After Charlie Anderson's decision to put me on probation, I was not altogether surprised. I knew at some level that my youthful energy was stagnating, despite the renewed energy I had felt in those days. Still, it was devastating news, so I called Morlean to ask advice. Despite the fact that we were no longer married, she was glad to hear my voice and offered me some sage advice. She said, "Leave others alone and lighten up".

In 1999, the surviving three companies that made up the Factory Mutual System agreed to a merger. I was informed that I was no longer going to be the senior engineering executive in the System. I was offered a job of leading the Learning from Losses Program that I had created. I turned down the offer and chose the early retirement route.

Had I taken a deep breath, swallowed my pride and considered the pluses and minuses for a few days, including the financial benefits of staying until I turned sixty-two, I would have stuck it out for three more years. However, my reactivity and pride got the best of me when I made a poor decision and turned down the offer.

I recall, however, a certain satisfaction at the events that happened after I took the early retirement option. Allendale's Management Committee hosted a retirement party at the Hope Club in Providence. The Engineering Managers held at party at Twenty Water Street, on Greenwich Bay. Daniel and Leslie joined the managers. My retirement gift was unbelievably creative. It was a 27 x 22 inch Factory Mutual engineering plan from 1927, signed by twenty seven of my fellow FM System engineers and executives, with each signature attaching a salutary message of congratulations and best wishes. I received a stackful of cards and congratulatory letters from as far away as Melbourne, Australia and Germany. All of this attention reaffirmed that I mattered and had made a major difference in many lives. What could be a better send off.

Of all the decisions I have made in my life, my immediate and hearty "yes" to the job opportunity of transferring to our foreign operations in London, was the most valuable and rewarding. For our good fortune, I offer the following selfie testimonial from the Wauwatosa Anglophile: "I hereby acknowledge my prescience, intuition, vision, determination, courage and can-do attitude that gave me the strength to fulfill my eight-year-overseas assignment in spades. As a Brit might put it, "I was bloody brilliant".

When I look back over my steady advancement through the ranks, it was my commitment and dedication to the loss prevention mission of the Factory Mutual System, and my steadfast determination to do the right things right at all costs, that explains much my success. I believed in the mission and gave it my all.

I never, for one moment in my thirty-five-year career, sought out raises, promotions or another more lucrative job. I did my job and my superiors did theirs. Low and behold, success arrived organically. Mine is a rich and compelling story with universal applications. I have always thought of myself as just another kid, teen, guy, dad, husband, granddad or bloke. I have always seen, heard and treated all human beings as equals. Lastly, nary a day goes by that I do not acknowledge the solid foundation my parents provided and the sacrifices they made on my behalf.

15

New England Patriots

In 1992, no one in their wildest fantasies could predict what the forthcoming twenty-six years would bring for the Patriots. My son Daniel shared my enthusiasm, and we were fortunate to live in Norfolk, Massachusetts in the same neighborhood where the team practiced and team members Steve Grogan, Don Hasselbeck and native Englishman placekicker John Smith lived. John and I shared memories of England. Our second exposures were at the Patriots 1983 summer camp at Bryant College, in Smithfield, RI. Daniel and I would hang on the fence and gawk as the exhausted players slunk by on their way to the locker room. Autographs were easy to get.

The Patriots have an interesting history, one that newer fans might not know. The original 1960 team was named the Boston Patriots and they played at several stadiums before Foxboro Stadium came along in 1971. When the team joined the NFL in 1970, its name was changed to the New England Patriots. They played their games at Foxboro Stadium from 1971 - 2001, before moving to Gillette Stadium in 2002. That same year, my oldest grandson, Benjamin Peacock became the first eleven month old to attend a Pat's night game at Gillette Stadium.

In 1996, I offered to host Daniel, Leslie and my wife Deb at one Patriot away game each. Daniel chose the Pats-Cowboys. It was so cold *inside* the stadium that I had to buy a heavy Cowboy's sweatshirt.

Deb chose the Pats-San Diego game. Prior to the game, we toured the city and I managed to slip in a downtown 5K road race. We extended our stay with two nights at the Hilton La Jolla Torrey Pines Hotel, which overlooks the renowned the twin Torrey Pines Golf Courses. I played both the north and south courses. What was unique about the courses is that a forecaddie was provided for the first two holes to help strangers find their tee shots and keep things moving along. What a great idea!

Leslie chose the Pats-Denver night game in Mile High Stadium. The day following the game we visited the University of Colorado in Boulder as well as the exquisite United States Air Force Academy just north of Colorado Springs. Our drive through The Garden of the Gods in the "Springs" was topping on the beauty cake. My dad had often told the story of his driving to the top of Pikes Peak on his honeymoon in 1929. This was a true fete, considering the automobiles of that vintage.

Awareness and opportunism set the stage for a lasting relationship with the Patriots. One morning in 1998, I noticed a short paragraph in the Providence Journal announcing a meeting of Bob Kraft and his board. The purpose was the unveiling of the first glimpse of what the planned Gillette Stadium might look like. As I had established a relationship in the Patriots Ticket Department, I called my guy to find out when and where the meeting would be held. At the announced time and date, I joined the formal meeting of Bob Kraft, his oldest son Jonathan, his board members, Willie McGinest, Ty Law and Drew McQueen Bledsoe. No one seemed to notice that I had no business being there, nor my casual dress. Could they have mistaken me for a waiter taking drink orders?

I got my autographs, photos and copies of the conceptual drawings, out of which I created a collage that hung on my wall for ten years.

I name dropped about the meeting with my ticket contact and got his agreement to ship me the first tentative seating plans. True to his word, a copy arrived a few months later. The plan showed three seating options: traditional outdoor seating, an innovative *Club Seat* concept that included outdoor seats and high-end indoor facilities for dining, drinking, TV watching and fireplaces and traditional box seats.

Deb and I decided to treat ourselves to two club seats, for which I had to buy a ten-year package. With the advance copy of the seating possibilities from my contact, I chose two aisle seats in the eighth row, on the 35-yard line. In chilly or rainy weather, Deb canscoot inside and warm up by one of the many firesides. I could hit the john and be back in my seat before a timeout was over. For some games, we came early and had dinner in their dining section.

Looking back, we couldn't have made a wiser decision. As Club

Members we had the option of buying a package for their Super Bowls. The packages included transportation, hotel accommodations, game tickets, tickets for the Thursday and Saturday night parties with all the players except Brady.

When the ten-year contract for the club seats ended, we passed. I was seventy two, and the effort to attend games exceeded the reward, especially for night games which would get us home hours after my beddy-bye time. I sold the rights to the seats for a two thousand dollar profit. We remain avid fans and often dine on our fond memories of the three Super Bowls we attended.

Super Bowl XXXVI
Superdome (New Orleans)
February 3, 2002

> *"When Adam kicked after Brady passed, a super bowl was ours at last."*
> *Wayne Benjamin Peacock*

Club seat members were offered a $9,700 package that included the flights, three nights lodging, game tickets, and tickets to the Thursday and Saturday night parties. Ask either Deb or me and we will tell you story after story. I remember the three buses that drove us from Foxboro right onto the tarmac aside our waiting plane, having had every road to Logan Airport cleared of traffic. It was kind of eerie.

The Thursday night party was a hoot. Tedy Bruschi sat alongside our table trying to manage his first newborn son, Tedy Bruschi Jr. Willie McGinest played with his three young daughters nearby. We hobnobbed with the elite 'til the music stopped. The only player who was not at the party was Tom Brady. Knowing Tom, I speculated that he was concentrating on his game plan.

We learned that on Saturday night the team is closeted away at an undisclosed site far away from all distractions.

The once in a lifetime game came down to the final play in which Adam Vinatieri kicked the winning field goal.

New England Patriots 20, St. Louis Rams 17

My OMG moment came when Queens' "We are the Champions" played immediately following the win, *"We Are the Champions"*, brings tears to my eyes every time I hear it. The post-game party was a most joyous of celebrations.

The Radiant Stadium in Houston hosted Super Bowl XXXVIII, February 1, 2004

The package offered by the Patriots was too expensive for a retiree. However, Daniel found a woman at work that got us two tickets on the twenty seven yard line, first row. Jolly kind of her. Once again, a tied game came down to the final play, where Adam Vinatieri kicked the winning field goal.

New England 32 Carolina 29

Deb and I took advantage of the Patriots package for Super Bowl XXXVIII held in the Alltel Stadium in Jacksonville, Florida, on February 6, 2005. We were very glad we did. To be a super bowl host, a certain number of hotel rooms are needed, which Jacksonville did not have. So, what do you s'pose they did. They brought five ocean liners up the St. Johns River alongside the stadium. Our package put us on an ocean liner, a first for Deb. It was a blast. I played basketball on the very edge of the top deck where a netting was the only thing between me and a fourteen floor drop to the water.

Super Bowl Summary: The Pats have appeared in nine Super Bowls, the most of any NFL team. Seven of them have incurred since the arrival of Bill Belichick and Tom Brady. They have won fourteen AFC East titles in 16 seasons since 2001. They hold the record for the most super bowls reached by a coach-quarterback combination (seven) and won (five). They are tied with the 49ers and Cowboys for the second most Super Bowl wins with five, and behind the Steelers with six.

16
The World of Fine Arts

I was invited to be the best man for Bob Quarnstrom, my roommate at Michigan, in the spring of 1964. The eccentric in me was striving to find a unique gift. By happenstance, I stumbled across a rural art gallery where I met the owner, Irving Luntz, and his assistant, Franci Schoonfield. I spent that initial meeting engrossed with his descriptions of modern masters and contemporary art.

My nature, and deep curiosity is to ask lots of meaningful and often unorthodox questions. Irving's responses were gift-wrapped bundles of delightful information. He answered each question with the richness of a masterful lover of art and made me hungry for more. I didn't realize it at the time, but I was in the presence of a genius. Based on that one solitary hour, Irving qualified as a world class influencer in my life. The Luntz saga had just begun.

Throughout our conversation, Irving was looking around for a painting that would meet my requirements for the unusual, and would fit my pocketbook. A light bulb went on. He had a rather rare book for sale with two hundred eleven pages of brilliant Marc Chagall lithographs. One must page through the book to appreciate just how magical Marc was. And, the price of the book was a whopping twenty five dollars. I was sold on Irving's suggestion. Presciently sensing a priceless treasure, I bought four copies of the book. My propensity to seek a unique gift was richly rewarded. Chagall became a household name for art lovers and a favorite of mine.

Not surprisingly, my eccentric gift was a big hit with Bob and his wife Karen. It rested serenely on their living room coffee table for years until their house burned down, leaving the treasured book in ashes. Years later when I visited their new home, I brought them one of my remaining copies.

A few weeks later I returned to the gallery with the objective of seeing what else I could find. The visit yielded an adorable etching: "Striptease in Blue" by Miro, and a series of ten etchings named "Le Blanc et LeNoir" by Louis Marcoussis. I lost those keepsakes in my divorce settlement and was very sad.

I signed up for a Fourteenth Century Arts course at the University of Wisconsin-Milwaukee, and purchased the course book, *Italian Painting, 1200-1600*. One of the teacher's lectures focused on a Giotto masterpiece. Serendipitously on a visit to the Uffizi Gallery in Florence, I came face to face with Giotto's Madonna from Ognissanti, a panel painting measuring one hundred and twenty eight by eighty inches. Tears came to my eyes because it's beauty overwhelmed me.

On my next visit to the gallery, Irving could hardly wait to tell me that he had just returned from Paris with over seventy Picassos. He got my immediate attention. My first Picasso purchase was an original lithograph, "Still Life", a 4 x 6 inch, black and white, 1909 print from the early days of Cubism for $675. It was one of 75 copies. Next, I bought a beautiful 1938 colored print of a bowl of fruits for $350. It was one of 275 copies. Lastly, I bought an aquatint colored print: "Arena", of a classic bull fight. Regretfully, a few months later Irving asked if he could buy it back for the same price I paid. Catching me off guard, I capitulated.

A couple decades passed until the day I walked into The Irving Galleries on the posh Worth Avenue, in Palm Beach, Florida. I had gone off to London and Irving had matriculated from the rural gallery to a more fitting gallery on Wisconsin Avenue in Milwaukee, before landing on a street fit strictly for millionaires in Palm Beach.

I began the reunion telling him, "I've done OK with the Picassos, but what have you done for me lately?" I am thinking to myself that my $250 and $675 investments, may have increased in value eight times over. Shrewd as he was, Irving knew that underneath my inquiry was the desire to make another insanely successful investment. He told me that I did not need to buy anymore artwork, you have plenty.

After we had wandered back to his office and gotten comfortable, he revealed that the art world had evolved and that the best investments were now in the Master Photography arena. Collectors, museums and galleries were in hot pursuit of the heretofore ignored photographs.

photographs of the masters did not become collectibles until around 1870. He followed up by asking if I had seen his current show, *"Henri Cartier-Bresson Europeans"*? In 1955, Henri Cartier-Bresson had published The Europeans, a collection of photographs taken over a period of five years. I flipped through the book and was mesmerized. In a nanosecond, the combined forces of my greed and intuition, led to the purchase of not one, but four of Henri's masterpieces. The four gems garnished our dining room wall until our finances changed when I retired. We sold the four gems.

A decade or more passed before my next visit to Irving's gallery. This time his show was Brassie, the Bulgarian who photographed Paris at night. We loved the photography and had the funds to purchase three of his finest photos, including the fiftieth anniversary of Maxim's in Paris. Irving had a hard time parting with this prize because his wife had made a claim on it. These three photos hang in our abode but if you look closely, you will notice that the other two are photocopies. We had to sell the photos to balance our budget.

Years later when our finances had improved, we read about Sotheby's "Fall Auction of Fine Arts" in New York City, so we drove down the prior weekend to get the lay of the land we knew nothing about. No surprise that I fixated on the infamous Pablo Ruiz Picasso. Pablo was a Spanish painter, sculptor, printmaker ceramicist, stage designer, poet and playwright who spent most of his life in France. He was probably the most important figure of the 20th century, in terms of art and art movements. We bought the catalog for the auction with photos of the most valuable sales items. The catalog itself became a Peacock keepsake.

We found a classic Cezanne that was estimated to go for from $6,000-8,000. Over the week that followed, we decided that we would go as high as $10,000. When the time came for our Cezanne, the bidding went from $6,000 to $14,000 in ten seconds. Not giving up, we won the auction for a priceless Picasso *Terre de faience* plate, 1963. We also came away with a Georges Rouault, *Paysage a la Tour* (C.'R.281) Aquatint, 1938, Edition of 250, 12 x 14 inches.

17 Road Racing

Road racing has been my identity for thirty eight years. Road racing was a giant magnet pulling me in. I went ever so willingly. No other activity, physical or mental, has had a more positive influence on my health and happiness than competitive running. The road racing community was and will remain my tribe.

The pre-race activities, the competitive nature of the race itself and the post-race experiences are what attracted me to become a road racer. Road running is the sport of running on a measured course over an established road as opposed to track and field and cross country. Races typically range from 5 Kilometers, 3.1 miles, to 42.2 kilometers; the 26.2-mile distance of a marathon. Once I discovered the sport of road racing, I was hooked. I may have been addicted at some point, whatever negative connotation that might imply. From 1978 to the present, I have run over eight hundred road races of distances varying from 1 to 26.2 miles. Just like tennis was my earlier identity, road racing became my new identity.

There is more than meets the eye when you consider becoming a runner or upping you level of running. Like all endeavors, it is wise to begin by asking yourself what you want to get out of running. Do I want to lose weight? Will it help me clear my mind after a hard day of mental concentration? Or do I simply appreciate the camaraderie of running with a fellow club member or two.

I discovered early on that there is an art to buying the right running shoes. I bought my running shoes at a running store where the salespersons were experienced runners. I tried on several labels, as each company's shoes are distinct. When I purchased shoes, I was assured that even after a month of use, my running stores allowed me to exchange them and for a pair that fit perfectly. I write the purchase date on the tongue of the shoe to help me track of how long I have been wearing them. I mention that because, in spite of my not noticing any difference as my shoes age, the innards of the shoes have a life expectancy. In my prime, I bought two pairs at a time so that I could wear a fresh pair on every run. My engineering logic informed me that whether I bought one pair of shoes twice or two pairs at a time, the cost will be the same in the long run, pun not intended.

After I retired from Allendale Insurance, I became a Professional Certified Coach, PCC. One of my first clients was a woman named Jackie Hennessy. One day while having tea together, and seeing my Brooks running shoes, it dawned on her that she had a friend that worked for Brooks at their main office in the state of Washington. It was serendipity because her connection afforded me a thirty percent discount on all of my shoe and gear purchases after that.

For my races, I purchased a pair of racing flats that were seven ounces lighter. I swore by them once I noticed the difference a few ounces made. After I solved my shoe needs, I built up a runners wardrobe so that I would look and feel like an experienced and stylishly runner. I purchased gear appropriate for all weather and temperature conditions. I did so online and at local running stores.

I have always worn knee straps as a preventive measure and have never had any knee problems over the thousands of miles I have run. The specialists I spoke to told me that in all likelihood concluded that knee straps act as inexpensive prevention.

If you have knee issues, the specialists I spoke to told me that in all likelihood the cause originates below your knees. Eventually I found a podiatrist who specialized in fitting athletes with their shoes. In my case, prescription inserts were needed to provide the right support.

When racing, I pin my number to my shorts in case I want to remove my top; which I frequently do, and especially in the heat of the summer. I doubt if this tip will have any value for my women friends.

I think *layers* when it is cold. The older I become, the more layers I need to be warm and comfortable; especially because I don't carry much fat. Sometimes, one or more of those layers gts left in the car after I have warmed up for a race.

At some point I began taking a new energy gel on the market with the cleaver name of GU. GU is very popular for long distance races. Even now, at eighty-years-old, I take a GU before my infrequent races.

In 2017, I bought a pair of red and a pair of blue shoes. It is not unusual to find me wearing one red and one blue. I make up that you always want to wear something that gives introverts an excuse to start a conversation with me, an eccentric extrovert.

My most recent shoes, the Brooks Asteria, double as a training shoe and racer. Too bad I am hardly racing anymore.

The Sunday Times National Fun Run – London

The first race I ever ran was in England on October 1, 1978. The roughly 2.3-mile fun run was held in the historic Hyde Park. This inaugural run at once became the biggest participatory sporting event ever held in Great Britain. Thousands of all ages ran as did my wife Morlean, my 17-year-old son Christopher, my ten-year-old daughter Leslie and my 7-year-old son Daniel. I finished 174th out of 824 males in the 40-49 age group. Morlean placed 239th out of 347. Leslie placed 89th out 178 in the Girls under 15. Daniel placed 295th out of 304. All four of us were impressive in our respective gender and age groups. And to top it off the Peacocks placed 17th of 36 in the Two Generation Teams event.

To be precise, I could also make the case that my first true road race occurred one year later with a ten-mile race in Wimbledon, not far from our home in Putney Heath. A week later I managed another 10-mile race just before we returned to the USA in the summer of 1979. It is interesting to note that my first two road races were ten 10 milers, no small task. It suggests that my life-long marginal propensity to run just for the sake of running had me in very good cardio condition.

The two London road races gave birth to the sport that met my cardio and competitive needs. First of all, I did not need a running partner, coach, running club or any outside assistance. I got along fine with just the *Runner's World* magazine. I could run anytime, day or night, in the summer heat and the cold of the winter. I could find a place to run from any location. With hindsight, the thousands of miles run and raced were the best gift I could have given my body and mind. As a bonus, the cardio exercise was the perfect antidote for the mental intensity that I brought to my career as a global loss prevention engineer.

Arriving back in the USA, and settling in Norfolk, MA just outside of Boston, it did not take long to realize that we lived plump in the middle of the fast-growing sport of road racing, with Boston as its mecca. Running legends from the area Johnny Kelly, Frank Shorter and Bill Rodgers come quickly to mind.

One of the first things I did was look for information about road races. I quickly found an announcement for a local 10K race. This, my first 10K race, went well. Road racing was perfect in that I was free to find my own way: how often to race, how hard to train, how serious to take it and what goals to set.

Between that first 10K road race and the recent past, I have run over 800 road races of all shapes, sizes, descriptions and conditions, from one milers all the way to four 26.2-mile marathons. A sampling of Hall of Fame like road racing experiences follows.

First Boston Marathon – Norfolk

Growing up I saw the marathon as a near impossibility. That I might run twenty-six point two miles never entered my mind; much less walk that far. Neither was a marathon on my bucket list because I did not know what a "bucket list" was until my late middle age.

To qualify for my first Boston, I needed to have had run a marathon in the previous year in under 3:10 minutes. I decided that I would use the Foxboro Marathon which was two weeks prior to Boston.

It was taken as gospel from *Runner's World Magazine* that one should run three twenty milers in preparation for a 26.2-mile marathon. My first goal was to increase my weekly mileage up to thirty miles a week, which I did. My next goal was to run the three twenty milers. Taffy, our American Cocker Spaniel, accompanied me on the first two of those twenty milers. He was an immense help in that he would distract me from my discomfort. I would take a short break halfway through for him to slurp the water I had arranged ahead of time.

My third twenty-miler had a story. I saw that The Ocean Run Marathon in Newport was scheduled for the third weekend prior to Boston so I got the creative notion that I would run the first twenty miles for my third twenty miler. This was wise because it is far easier to run with hundreds of others then it is all alone with your temptation to quit increases as the discomfort increases. So I did, and a strange thing happened when I got to the twenty-mile marker. I decided that since I was this far, and my dream was to complete a marathon, I would just keep on running to see if I could finish, which I did with a great deal of pride and satisfaction.

Next on the docket was the Foxboro Marathon where I needed to score a 3:10 time to qualify. I finished the uneventful 26.2 mile race in 3:15 and submitted my application to Boston with my fingers crossed that they would find it in their heart to overlook my five minutes over the limit. Sure enough, I was accepted much to my glee.

With great excitement I went to the starting line in Hopkinton with an estimated 6,500 others. The temperature a foot above the road was over 100 degrees. A helicopter overhead heightened the tension and I cried when the star-spangled banner was sung.

By the ten-mile mark I was really feeling the heat. I was still feeling OK until the beginning of the infamous "heartbreak" hills. My first memory of the hills was passing a wheelchair racer. As I passed, I touched him on the shoulder and said something like, "Way to go, guy". I broke out in tears the moment my fingers hit his body. As an aside, I am always impressed by the determination and endurance required of a wheelchair racer.

The closer I got to the finish line the more often I would hear, "Only X miles to go". The problem with this well intentioned support was that almost all were inaccurate on the wrong side, meaning it was always further than they said. Next Boston in my afterlife, I will use ear plugs for the final stretch.

I finished in 00:03:27 minutes and almost collapsed on my feet while some others were sprawled on the ground. I made my way to the basement locker room of the Prudential Building, where I spent the next half hour on my back under a shower. Surviving runners littered the place so much so that it looked like a war scene. Somehow, I got myself to a restaurant near the FM Hotel in Norwood where I was booked. My body could not have been more miserable. When I went to take another warm shower at the hotel there was no hot water. The custodian, a fellow employee of Factory Mutual, was ever so empathetic for my suffering without a hot shower. For the remaining time I worked at FM, every time our paths crossed we would lament the 1980 cold water event.

Second Boston Marathon - Hudson, Ohio

With a return to normal temperatures, I finished in 00:03:04 and change. It became my PB, personal best, for Boston.

The Frosty Five Classic on New Year's Day is perhaps the most scenic race in little Roady. It runs along east Bristol Harbor into Colt State Park with Narragansett Bay on the right before returning along the Harbor to the finish line. My last trophy from this race had a

Narragansett Beer can topped with a running figure. You will return home just in time to watch three bowl games.

Blessing of the Fleet - 10 Miler

The Narragansett Lions Club held its first (one day) Blessing of the Fleet in the summer of 1972. The Blessing included three events: Seafood Festival, 10 Mile Road Race and Blessing of the Fleet. In 2017, the Blessing was expanded to 3 days. These ten milers are always well attended, and for many runners this is their only race of the year.

Gaspee Days 5K

The three-day Gaspee Days Arts & Crafts Festival showcases the works of artisans, community groups and nonprofits, and is a well attended Pawtuxet tradition. In June of 1772, brave colonists from Rhode Island burned the British revenue schooner, HMS Gaspee, in what has become recognized as the first overt action leading up to the American Revolutionary War. For the past 65 years, the village of Pawtuxet, has commemorated this act with its annual Gaspee Days Celebration. It is one of the most exciting and patriotic parades in the country, featuring colonial life and drum corps, Civil War era units, modern day drum and bugle corps and much more.

This popular road race has kicked off the brilliantly colorful festival for thirty six years. In 2018, the race attracted 1660 runners, most of whom were dressed up in red, white and blue. I walked and jogged the race in 41 plus minutes. The oldest age group was 60 and over so I as a 79 year old competing against 60 year olds. Now that is just not fair, is it? I walked to the car empty handed. Then a debilitating three hour saga began when I could not find my car. I walked around for 90 minutes with no luck. Eventually I called the Warwick police who came and drove me around some more. Then the police called Deb so she could pick me up at the Warwick Police Station, which she did. She insisted on retracing the territory surrounding the race course a few more times, without any luck. By this time I had been walking for three hours in sunny 86 degree weather in my damp, post race gear. Besides, my sockless feet were aching. Reluctantly, Deb called it a day and I slept rather soundly. The phone rang the next morning with the news that the policeman who had driven me around looking for the car, had found the car in the place where I had forgotten I parked it.

There is an explanation for the forgetfulness. In 2014, I suffered a serious head trauma with a concussion as a result of tripping just after I got out of my car. I crash landed on my chest and face/head. Since that "head meets concrete" trauma, I have been handicapped because my short term memory has been problematic. When I get stressed my head feels warm, my mind gets confused, I forget simple facts I just heard and I lose my sense of distance and direction. For example, before the trauma if I went to my doctors office several miles away I could envision the entire route. That is no longer true. most often I am totally dependent on my iPhones' mapping. There have been several situations resulted in being lost for a few hours, some of the scary nature.

CVS Downtown

I think this is the best attended road race in RI, save for the Blessing of the Fleet, maybe. The race includes the New England Women's 5K Championship. The fast course runs through downtown Providence and finishes with a slightly uphill finish. The race is followed by a lively band, and bananas and other post race goodies for all.

St. Patrick's Day 5K

This race is one in a series of three races that celebrate St. Patrick. The tee shirts that accompany the races are superior in design and quality compared to typical cotten road race tees. In the first year of the series, I won all three races. My reward was a tee specially designed for a winner of all three races. In 2018, I jogged-walked the three races and have four beautiful tees to show for it.

My road racing career was filled with highlights and a few significant injuries, as would be expected of someone who has run an estimated 20,000 miles. My earliest injury was Plantar Fasciitis, which is very painful and takes months to rid one self of. Some thirty years later, undiagnosed atrial-fibrillation (AFib) began to impact my breathing and thus my results. The fingers-crossed fix for AFib is a cardioversion, a procedure for which I'm anesthetized, after which my heart is shocked with a couple hundred joules. The cardioversion held for only three months, so another cardioversion was called for. The second cardioversion lasted four months. My current cardioversion has lasted six months and fingers crossed. Maybe it because I am not running very much.

A few years later I was walking with a cane in greater and greater pain in my left hip. Fast forward to April 8, 2014, when I had a complete hip replacement that went like clockwork. There was a video of me being loopy and happy while still anesthetized two hours after the surgery. That first day they taught me how to walk with crutches. The second day they taught me how to walk upstairs with the crutches. Later that day I was released and on my own. An RN came daily to check my vitals and assist as needed. I continued to heal and at twenty days was filmed hitting golf balls in the backyard. There was another video of me jogging around the East Greenwich HS track at about eighty-five days. At 117 days, I jogged and walked a 5K road race and finished in forty nine minutes. My wife Deb, was pleased because she finally beat me in a 5K road race.

18

Posits

My eightieth birthday was celebrated on July 23rd, with my family and friends. Their presence filled me with joy and gratitude. I felt blessed. My heart goes out to all those who had an elder birthday alone.

Eighty years is a l—o—n—g time. Throughout those years I have witnessed the first man on the moon, neverending manmade wars, both trustworthy and fraudulent politicians, gluttonous wealth, horrendous natural and human disasters, awe inspiring athletic performances, technological advances in education, healthcare and manufacturing, and charities fighting world poverty across the shrinking globe.

My positivity and confidence in the universe is continuously being tested by the in-your-face racism, misogyny and other isms, along with the brutal treatment of migrants and immigrants in our land of the free on television every day.

My better self tells me that this too will pass and that courage and love will triumph over evil.

I want to be remembered for the positivity and inspiration I exude as well as my double- entendre sense of humor.

I also want to be remembered for my continuous effort and dedication to the pursuit of optimum wellness.

My greatest gift to my family and friends is that they have always known they are loved as they are and are not.

Go Blue and Go Pats

19
The Epilogue

I began writing this autobiography at the age of seventy eight and will finally complete it at the ripe old age of eighty when my gifted editor finally runs out of things to correct or enhance. It includes ninety pages with 38,700 words and 176,078 characters.

Without any outline or planning I began typing away on my new personal computer with it's wonderful twenty one by nine-inch screen propped up five inches on a stand and a detached keyboard. The computer resides in my ever-so-homey office surrounded by bookshelves, a reading chair and footrest, a cross legged stone buddha on the floor, keepsake pictures on the walls and my most revered trophy for outstanding leadership on a wooden storage cabinet. My office resides in our 1300 sq. ft. first floor apartment in a complex of six hundred and thirty Briarwood Meadows apartments.

Driven by my Enneagram One trait, I wrote it as well as I could and continuously improved it. I worked conscientiously to learn from the editing and my self assessments. I learned so much from Google everyday.

By far the smartest thing I did was to create a timeline for each of the sixteen linear elements. My first element began when I started following the Green Bay Packers on the radio in 1948 as a ten- year-old. I looked to the timeline countless times each day to get my time and spacial bearings. I am having an artist create a replica for my wall and possible insertion in the book.

My fact-based engineering mind comes through in the script as does my desire to say it like it was.

The longer I wrote, pondered over options, googled, was edited and wrote some more, the more I held autobiographical writing as a discrete art form with unlimited options. Besides the challenge of accurately recalling my past, I had to perceptively recall who I was and how I created my own destiny.

"While I was mostly always driving the train, I was also being magically transported by the train ride."
Authored by: Wayne Hafiz Rumi

ACKNOWLEDGEMENTS

Celia Taylor was the ideal editor for me. She was timely and reliable. She met me where I was. She pointed out areas that were worthy of more explanation, depth and alignment. Her poignant, open ended questions often lead me to new and more relevant destinations. Her way of being with me was impeccable. She allowed me to ramble on regardless of any relevance to the book. I appreciated her occasional laudatory comments. For example, finding an "interesting" in the margin would make my day, and sometimes my week.

My wife Debbie has quietly supported my fifteen month adventure in biography writing and chipped in on my spelling inquiries.

I got plenty of on-going support and interest from friends and acquaintances who all want to know when they will be able to buy an autographed copy.

ABOUT THE AUTHOR

With the clock ticking, the time arrived for Wayne to pass on the essence of his being in a linear biography.

Wayne was a Great Depression baby who grew up in the blissful suburb of Wauwatosa.

His prowess and achievements across a variety of sporting activities speaks to his high level of athleticism.

His pursuit of a Mechanical Engineering degree from the **University of Michigan** insured a blue-ribbon education.

His thirty-five-year career in loss prevention engineering propelled him to the pinnacle of global executive leadership.

His career called for thousands of written reports and in retirement he has flourished as an eccentric writer of newsletters, blogs and columns.

The International Coach Federation conferred the designation of Professional Certified Coach on Wayne.

In the spiritual realm, he identifies himself as a non-secular humanist and atheist.

His work, play and travel over six decades in twenty three countries on five continents has cultivated a comprehensive and compassionate worldview.

He boastfully claims that life begins at eighty. We'll see how that turns out.

A Man for All Seasons, is an apt description.

Made in the USA
Middletown, DE
20 August 2021